WATER FEATURES
for small gardens

WATER FEATURES
for small gardens

ETHNE CLARKE

WARD LOCK

A WARD LOCK BOOK

First published in the UK 1998
by Ward Lock
Wellington House
125 Strand
LONDON
WC2R 0BB

A Cassell Imprint

Distributed in the United States
by Sterling Publishing Co., Inc.
387 Park Avenue South, New York, NY 10016–8810

Distributed in Canada
by Cavendish Books Inc.
Unit 5, 801 West 1st Street
North Vancouver, B.C. Canada V7P 1PH

A British Library Cataloguing in Publication Data block for this book may be obtained from the British Library

Technical Consultant: Peter Robinson

ISBN 0 7063 7706 0

Designed and typeset by Les Dominey
Illustrations by Pond and Giles
Colour wheel by Dawn Brend
Printed by Wing King Tong Co., Hong Kong

CONTENTS

INTRODUCTION

Modern materials, like these glass tubes and coloured glass pebbles, make a distinctive fountain. The brimming columns of water bubble and froth within the confines of the tubes, making the fountain particularly well suited to a small garden.

Small gardens, especially those in towns, pose specific problems to aspiring gardeners, and one of the most frequently confronted puzzles is what can be done to make the little space more interesting. Colourful flower borders have tremendous appeal in the summer, but to devote a large chunk of the garden to a one-season show is not practical, and there is often not the space to include many shrubs as well to prolong the interest. Paving and containers are a favourite antidote to limited space, but then the pot-grown garden can become rather static, and in winter can make the garden look like a clear-out in a potting shed.

A small water feature, however, can offer a solution. Many of the ones described in this book would bring year-round interest to a small garden and can be styled to fit into any kind of garden scene – formal arrangements of pools and sculpted fountains, informal ponds to encourage wildlife and bring a slice of rural calm into an urban setting. Other ideas include tranquil reflecting ponds, Oriental-style water spouts, even a half-barrel transformed to accommodate a specimen water plant or cherished goldfish. And no matter what the season or the setting, water brings an unquantifiable quality to a garden.

Small water features, of course, are not confined to small plots. A water spout tipping into a tiny moss-edged pool in a shady corner of a large garden has all the more appeal for not being scaled up to the proportions of the whole garden. I have always wanted a water feature in my garden and so it is a source of mild irritation that the previous owner of our place filled in the farm pond. By all accounts, it had a lovely willow tree over-hanging it, and I envisaged it with irises, rodgersias, skunk cabbage, candlestick primulas and marginal plants dappling its edges.

So determined was I to have water, that one of my neighbours volunteered to dowse. He arrived with a forked hazel twig and began marching up and down the as yet un-gardened field. Finally Basil stopped, the twig jerked downwards. 'Here,' he said, 'and here,' pacing on a few more steps. 'And here too!' My excitement was hard to contain – all that water just waiting to be made into a stunning garden feature.

'Only trouble is, I can tell you that it's here, but what I can't tell you is how far down and it could be a very long way!'

So that was the end of my great ornamental pool, but now I delight in a tub of waterlilies and a rather damp spot where I can cosset the moisture-loving plants that interest me most.

Elsewhere in the garden I have dreams of installing a reflecting pool, but I don't imagine it will be one of those grand architectural, Edwin Lutyens-style affairs, with smart stone edging, set in the middle of an emerald lawn. This will be much more homespun and copied from my friend Constance (whose family really does own a Lutyens house and garden). In her own cottage garden in Normandy, she set a flat concrete paving slab in the lawn, built up an edging of sea-smoothed stones and old red bricks, and mortared them in place leaving a small well in the centre. Here rainwater collects, or she tops it up with tapwater during dry spells. Dinky frogs leap in and out, dragonflies are attracted by the delicate glitter of the few cupfuls of water it holds, and tiny yellow violets and primroses are reflected in its miniature mirrored surface. Big is beautiful, but small and perfectly formed serves just as well! And what attracts me most about this particular water feature is that it can be made to serve any size of garden, and is supremely low-tech – even I can mix mortar and collect stones.

A small garden can always be enhanced by an appropriate water feature. Here, a terracotta pot containing Nymphoides peltata, *surrounded by lush foliage, makes a rustic effect.*

WATER
for effect

Japanese gardens are constructed as symbols of the natural world. Here a gravel 'island' supports a specimen Pinus mugo, *and is ornamented with a traditional deer-scarer, the* shishi odoshi.

Water shapes our world, defining continents, etching valleys and contouring the hillsides with rills and cascades. Waterfalls and white water rapids remind us of the power of nature and the fact that without water we would not have life – even plants in the driest regions depend on the most meagre annual rainfall for their existence.

Water gardens past and present

If we think about our garden as a small world within the grander scheme of things, wherein are represented all the elements of life, then we should by rights make every effort to include a water feature, however small, to make that world complete.

Nowhere is this thought more evident than in the traditional Japanese garden. In the west, our gardens have generally been made to reflect our dominance of nature (only lately has the ecological garden come into fashion); the Japanese garden exists to remind the viewer that they are a participating member of nature's family, and thus each element of the garden is a reminder of that fact. Water is one of the prime elements of nature/life, and so no Japanese garden will be complete without water, even if it is only present as a ribbon of river pebbles representing a dry riverbed.

The Japanese garden has long been a rich hunting ground for landscape designers searching for a new expression of familiar features. Translating such a profound cultural statement as the Japanese garden can result in some equally profound misunderstandings, primarily because we do not have the same aesthetic sense of the natural world as the Japanese. But we can learn, and adapt, and enjoy the extra dimension that water brings.

In the west our gardening traditions had their origins in the Islamic garden, where formal canals bisected a garden plot planted with fruit trees and scented flowers. Water was the symbol of life in this microcosmic *pairidaeza* (the Persian word for 'park'), for the early Islamic gardens were created out of an arid, barren landscape where water was the scarcest and most precious commodity. Returning Crusaders brought their experience of Islamic culture, and gardens, to Europe. Possibly the most famous surviving Islamic gardens are in the Alhambra in Granada, Spain, where avenues of jets send up elegant arches of spray and the sun-baked enclosed courtyards seem cooler for the sight and sound of tinkling fountains. The Persians' *pairidaeza* became in English 'paradise', our oldest word for an ornamental garden.

Water games

Water is more than the source of life – as if that were not enough! It is a source of fun, of serenity and relaxation, of joy, curiosity and of mystery.

There is a public park in Paris built on the site of the old Citroën car factory, and called the Parc André Citroën. It opened in 1993, and the system of cascades, canals and jet fountains around which the park has been planned surpasses any since the monumental water gardens at the Villa D'Este at Tivoli outside Rome were built during the sixteenth century. The centrepiece of the waterworks at the Parisian park is the water-jet terrace; the rise and fall of each jet is orchestrated by computer program to give a random pattern. One minute the jets are gushing like geysers, the next they fall flat, only to resume, tentatively at first, but gathering strength until once again they spurt three metres or more in the air. The local children race in and out of the display, challenging the jets to catch them if they can, stopping to place a rubber ball over a still nozzle to watch as it is lifted, spinning wildly in the erupting jet.

Giochi d'acqua, water games, were a popular feature in the gardens of Renaissance Italy and usually involved hidden jets and taps which were turned on while the unsuspecting garden visitor admired some plant or other – a bit like the squirting-flower buttonhole joke.

This wall-mounted fountain has a rather witty effect as pump-circulated water trickles from the 'overturned' bottle into the stone cistern below.

Resembling a waterfall, a gap in the wall's coping allows water to spill on to slate and gravel. The glitter of cascading water adds movement to the garden scene.

Right: *A bubble fountain breaks through a carefully arranged collection of smooth pebbles. The water highlights the colour and texture of the pebbles, adding another design element to the garden.*

It is the quality of surprise, of being caught unawares, that makes a water joke successful, so while you may not be able to create computerized pneumatic fountains, you can make a visual water joke from something unusual or unexpected. One of my all-time favourites is a watering can turned into a fountain by plumbing a water pipe into the can – the water it 'pours' is then collected in a basin to be pumped round once again. Set on a wall and sprinkling down in to the garden, it creates a nice moist atmosphere for wall-grown filmy-type ferns and other plants that relish the damp air.

Reflections and rhythms

Serenity and relaxation are pleasing qualities in a garden, and one of the surest ways to attain a meditative atmosphere is to include a still water feature – a tranquil pool situated in a quiet corner where the surrounding plantings are limited to peaceful greens and soft textures.

Still water has its own fascination – there is the mystery of ink-dark wells, silent pools, damp grottoes, sinuous rivulets that disappear beneath the rocks to emerge as a silvery film of water – but it is the sound of water that brings it to life. Some gardeners are lucky enough to have natural streams running through their gardens, or else forming one of the perimeter edges. Usually this will be in a rural setting, and a country garden decked out with a primrose-strewn bank above an iris-lined brook is some gardeners' idea of horticultural heaven. I love the scene conjured up by some country villages, where the stream runs across the front of the property and must be crossed to enter the garden. It gives the house and garden a

moated effect, and to pause for a moment enjoying the sight and sound of the flowing water enhances the sense of delight in the cottage garden beyond.

A similar effect can be achieved by situating an artificial stream across the front access to your house and using broad paving stones to make steps across the stream to the front door. Keep surrounding planting to a minimum – a fine specimen hosta like 'Sum and Substance', or other structural plants like arum lilies or the bold ostrich-feather fern (*Matteuccia struthiopteris*) – would reinforce the drama of such an entrance.

Most suburban front gardens would not provide a sympathetic setting for such scene, however, but there are other ways of introducing the musicality of water into the garden. A millstone with a small bubble fountain frothing up through the centre takes up no room at all and can be immensely pleasing to watch and listen. Two small scale ponds, one set slightly above the other and equipped with a small pump, will provide a pretty cascade as the water tumbles from one to the other.

A sheet of still water bisects a small garden, effectively breaking up the space into two separate areas. It also causes a physical break in the path so that you have to step carefully on to the paver to continue a pleasant stroll through the garden.

The capacity for water to make joyful music has for centuries been exploited by garden designers, never more so than during the Renaissance when the force of water was used to cause organs to play, statues to groan and pipes to whistle; the Villa d'Este mentioned earlier includes one vast fountain and cascade that plays a large water organ; its booming and whirring can be heard throughout the garden.

Sound must be carefully managed so as not to seem hectic or annoying; the slow, uneven trickle of a slight stream through a rockery, or the bright sparkle of a fountain can take time to achieve. Without the right combination of pump volume and landscaping, it can sound like nothing more than a tap left running. Experiment with breaking the pattern of flowing water

A naturalistic planting of purple loosestrife (Lythrum salicaria *'Firecandle'), inula, astilbes, ferns and willows is typical of the plant life that borders a natural stream.*

so that it becomes random and not a monotonous gush; it is astonishing what a difference a couple of carefully placed rocks can make. By adjusting the flow rate on a pump, a fountain can become a light-catching spray rather than a fierce geyser or a weak trickle, and check out the ever-widening range of nozzles for different effects (see pages 32–3).

Water wildlife

For many the main reason to create a water feature is not as an architectural focal point, or for the fascination of reflected light, nor yet for the musicality of flowing water, but for the wildlife it will attract – even my tub of waterlilies has dragonflies darting across it in the summer.

The planning for a small natural water feature in an urban or suburban garden can take you into local parks, neighbouring woodlands and heaths as you study what sort of habitat might once have existed in your now artificial environment. What sort of setting is most appropriate for the plants your soil type will support? And for the animals and insects you wish to attract? That way you will be certain to create something that the native wildlife will recognize and feel comfortable visiting. I think of my now-vanished farm pond and wonder if I should just exploit the natural sogginess of that filled-in corner to make a mini wetland garden. I know the local hedgehog community would enjoy the snails and slugs such a garden patch would doubtless attract! Remember, also, that you must allow access points where the border slopes gently into the water's edge, so that small mammals can safely drink without falling in, or if they do, they can clamber out without difficulty.

If you intend to focus on ornamental fish, you must also include plenty of water plants to provide them with oxygen and with shade. Fish do get sunburnt, so a good blanket of lily pads will provide welcome respite on a sunny day. On pages 64–5 is a project for creating a small wildlife pond.

DESIGN
considerations

There are numerous types of water garden features to choose from, to suit every dream and every pocket, from an all-in-one mask and basin fountain that you hang on a wall to a full-blown multiple cascade, pool and adjoining bog.

Cost, of course, is an important consideration, since water garden accoutrements can be pricey, but even a low-budget feature can prove a costly mistake if it is in the wrong place or jars with the rest of the garden, so it pays to spend a little time considering style, design and position.

STYLE

Because my garden is rural, and it is rather overgrown-cottage in style, I believe that a naturalistic pond would be most appropriate for the garden. Friends nearby, who have a large formal garden made in the grand Edwardian manner, have included a raised pool at the centre of a small cloister-type garden and a reflecting pool mysteriously hidden by close-set yew hedges within a sunken wall garden. In both cases the style of the

Two water features with very different characters: a circular pool is the focus of each but the restrained planting of camomile and ferns between the pavers around the brick-edged pool (left) provides a more restful contemplative mood than the abundantly planted pool (right) where the formal lines are blurred by plentiful foliage and flowers.

formal pool perfectly suits the spirit of the garden area
it graces.

Unless you are deliberately setting out to make a
surrealist garden, bear in mind that although the
garden is an artificial environment, you are striving to
create somewhere visually pleasing and harmonious,
where plants are at ease with each other and with their
setting. Any small water feature should also harmonize.

One of the most successful pools I know is the
circular bathing pool at Hidcote Manor Gardens in
Gloucestershire. When the garden was first laid out in
the early 1900s, the pool was a small circular dipping
well around which pie-wedge shaped beds revolved.
Later, the owner, Major Lawrence Johnston, decided
his guests needed somewhere to swim, so he enlarged the pool so it almost
entirely filled the yew-hedged enclosure. A path circumnavigates the pool,
and narrow flower beds hug the edges at the foot of the yew hedge. The
effect is quite enchanting, and could be mimicked in a town garden, allowing space for all manner of water plants to be grown, not to mention some
sizeable koi. Just because you have a limited space, doesn't mean you have
to think small (even though, as I said earlier, there is nothing wrong with
small). The great thing is to design and plant with conviction.

But your convictions must be well-informed; in other words – don't
think that to make a successful pond, for instance, all you have to do is
dig a hole, line it and fill up with water. The most common mistake I
encounter is when the pool has been sited at the top of a rise or slope,
and the spoil from the excavation is heaped around the perimeter. The
effect is that of a water-filled bomb crater ... and not at all natural, since
it is the nature of water to flow downhill and to settle at the lowest point
in the topography.

*A simple jet of water breaks the calm of
this asymmetrical yet formal pool, where
a calm, reflective quality is supported by
the simple container planting at the
pool edge.*

So, study the shape of your garden, assess its good and bad points and imagine the difference water might make: a small pool ringed with hostas on the terrace? A lion mask fountain on that wall? A raised pool in the lawn, with a fountain floodlit at night? If you live in a naturally hilly area, and you garden on the near vertical, a waterfall and rock pools would make a virtue out of difficult terrain. A craggy waterfall like this would lack credibility in a city-centre garden, but consider a stylized version, in the form of a water spout, perhaps contrived to spill out from a brimming urn.

In an urban setting a water feature forms part of the 'architectural' surroundings, rather than being any reflection of nature; its style could echo the period of the house or be the focus of an oasis designed to be the antithesis of the busy, noisy world outside. It might be a reflecting pool, set into the paving so that the water level exactly matches the level of the surround. Or a raised pool, like the one in my neighbours' cloister-style garden, could be constructed with the surrounding ledge broad enough for cushions, to become a convivial gathering place.

Pebbles and pots make ideal fountains where space is limited, allowing the intriguing vitality of moving water to be incorporated into the smallest of gardens.

Fountains, jets and other embellishments

Not every garden suits a classical spray fountain, although it is very tempting to try to incorporate one somewhere – they are pretty, they are fun and, carefully chosen and positioned, they can bring a water feature to life. It is also feasible to have some styles of fountain without a pool, which is an attractive idea if safety is a worry.

In a garden where there is a mass of colour and interest, a simple water spout may be more restful than a sophisticated spray pattern or an ornate fountain. Other water jet features include bubble fountains, emanating from either a basin or jar container, or else simply bubbling up from beneath a collection of rocks and pebbles. This type of display has an informal feel to it, and looks well in a cottage-style garden or tucked into a corner, where the water-washed pebbles look entirely natural.

If you have ever stood within range of a fountain on a blustery day, you will know what I mean when I advise that spray fountains be placed in sheltered spots in exposed gardens. If it isn't possible to organize this, then consider whether or not a bubble jet would be as effective and less likely to shower the surroundings.

The range of ornamental fountains, multiple head sprays and complex jets is increasing all the time (see pages 32–3 for more information); too often the difficulty is not finding what you want, but deciding from the huge range of possibilities.

LIGHTING

One of the last refinements to a water feature is added lighting. A well-positioned spotlight will enliven the pool at night, pick out the sparkle and play of moving water or illuminate a sculpted water feature. In a very small garden, lighting will make the most of what is probably your chief focal point, so that the garden doesn't lose all interest after nightfall. But do take care not to overdo it, and save the fairy lights and coloured bulbs for the Christmas tree. Plants and water look more subtle in subdued light and very often plain white light is the most effective.

A simple white submersible lamp adds greater mystery to the under-water scene. When planning to light a pond, avoid a broad white beam of light shining on to the water surface – the greatest effect is achieved from lighting when it creates new shadows and illusions different from those seen in daylight. You could consider objects or plants which seem to have less appeal in the day as potential highlights for lighting. This change of

Dramatic underwater lighting enhances the mask fountain in an elaborately terraced garden and emphasizes the attractive pattern of the tiling, making the fountain a focal point at night, when the garden might otherwise be ignored.

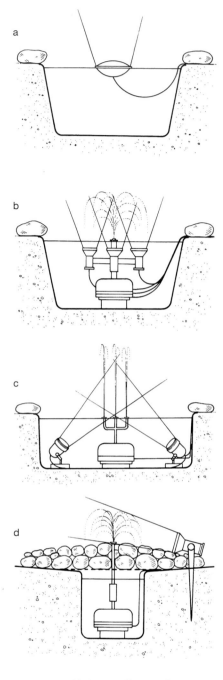

A variety of lighting effects: a floating spotlight (a); a fountain kit (b); submerged spots lighting a row of jets (c); and a landbased spot directed towards a cobble fountain (d).

emphasis on different subjects makes the garden more refreshing in the evening and draws out qualities of shape which may not have been apparent in daylight. When lighting a wall fountain, use a narrow spotlight which confines the light to the mask rather than covering a large area of wall behind as well.

Fountains are especially effective when lit from underneath or behind the fountain spray, catching and following the movement. Capture the simplicity of a cobble fountain by directing a concealed spotlamp directly on to the spout of water. The rhythmic gentle movement of a broad plume of illuminated water has a restful effect similar to the flames of a fire. In this instance an amber lens is a particularly effective colour choice.

As with lighting in a room, you may need to make several adjustments before the effect is entirely successful. Two final tips that may be helpful: avoid the light source shining towards the viewing point (unless it is angled upwards and diffused by a fountain spray or the tracery of fine branches), and choose lights with unobtrusive, matt casings – shiny white casings will be more difficult to conceal in daylight. The practicalities of installing lighting are explained on page 36.

SAFETY

A major consideration when deciding upon the type of water feature and its method of construction is safety. No matter how small or shallow the water, it will attract toddlers. Where small children have an area of garden where they play unattended it would be sensible to erect a temporary fence around open water which can be removed as the children grow. Where this is impractical, or the safety measures become so obtrusive that they spoil the effect, there are other steps you can take that will help to make a water feature safer provided children are not left unattended, at least when they are old enough to dismantle any safety measures.

Maximize the play element of moving water by covering the water surface

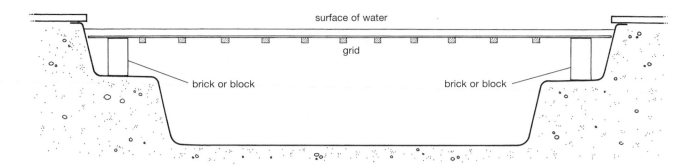

with a grid which supports cobbles (see the Raised Pool on pages 58–9.) A variety of spray patterns can be created through the cobbles which fascinate small children without endangering them. A wall fountain, like the Urban Cascade on pages 72–3, which spouts into a small pool covered by large pebbles at the base of the wall makes a good variation on a cobble fountain.

If you prefer to have an open water surface, make a simple safety grid which is supported on a shallow perimeter shelf just under the water surface, strong enough to support the weight of a child. A large-holed mesh of strong black plastic on a wooden frame is ideal as it is inconspicuous but also allows any marginal plants to grow through. This method is much less obtrusive than a fence around the pool.

A raised pool would be extremely difficult for a toddler to climb as long as it has a minimum height of 60cm (2ft) with slightly overhanging coping stones.

Make pool edges as safe as possible by:

◆ Heavy marginal planting (see pages 107 and 118–22)

◆ Shallow beaches

◆ Gentle gradients to the edge of the water, avoiding a steep slope down to the water

◆ Avoiding slippery surfaces at or near the edge. Old York stone paving slabs are notoriously slippery, whereas reconstituted stone or concrete paving slabs are available with non-slip surfaces.

◆ Ensuring any paving is stable around the edge by mortaring the slabs securely on to a firm base of hardcore. If any stones overlap the water ensure that there is no danger of them tipping when weight is concentrated at the edge of the water.

For safety, a grid can be supported on bricks or masonry blocks so that it is just below the surface of the water. A 2.5cm (1in) mesh attached to 7–8cm (3in) struts should be strong enough to support the weight of a child on a pool 2.4m (8ft) across.

POSITION

In a small garden you will not have many choices about position. If your intention is to cultivate a collection of water plants, to do well, they will require direct sunlight for a good part of the day during the growing season, so check where the shadows of walls, fences, trees, neighbouring houses and so forth fall. Trees close by will also present problems when they shed their leaves. Fallen leaves – and poisonous berries from shrubs like yew and laburnum – collecting in a pool will rot down, releasing noxious gases as they do, polluting the water and poisoning the fish.

When you have chosen what seems to be the best position, spread an old sheet on the ground or stick in a series of canes to represent the area of a pool, or use a bucket or dustbin to stand in for an ornamental statue, urn or barrel, and just look. Observe it as often as possible in changing weather and light conditions. Does it fit in well with the rest of the garden? Does it give the view you want from the house? Note where the sun rises and sets – evening sunshine behind a pool would make it an ideal site for a fountain.

You will also need to take into account the following practical considerations:

◆ *How level is the site?*

Although pools can be made on sloping sites, the construction will involve either cutting into the slope at the highest point of the gradient and making a small wall to retain the soil or raising the soil level at the lowest point and containing this with a raised wall. The overall design and contours of the garden may determine which to do, or the position of the house may influence your decision. If the house is looking uphill, then a retaining wall above the pool would be better so that the water can be seen more easily. Conversely, if the house is looking downhill, the

Opposite: *The running tap of water spilling continuously into the basin makes a moist atmosphere which will benefit a wide range of plants, including hostas, rodgersias and pulmonaria.*

A pool constructed on a slope must be cut into or built up from the slope. The direction from which the pool is viewed will determine the position of the retaining wall.

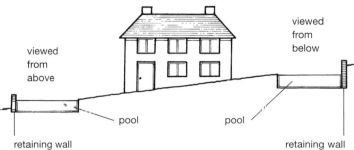

viewed from above

viewed from below

pool

pool

retaining wall

retaining wall

retaining wall or mound should be built on the lower side of the pool so that it is not seen from the house and your view of the pool is not obstructed.

◆ *Will any excavation avoid drains, gas mains and other services?*
It is relatively easy to pinpoint the route of mains drainage by examining the entry and exit points of the pipes in the sides of manholes. The routes of other services may not be so easy to identify and it is not uncommon for telephone and electric cables to be installed in a slight curve. The service suppliers will send engineers with specialist equipment to trace under-ground cables or pipes in the absence of any plans.

◆ *Is the site likely to flood or is pressure from ground water*
likely to cause a flexible liner to billow up?
Although the lowest part of the garden may seem to be the most obvious place to site an informal pool, on certain heavy soils the depth of under-ground water (the water table) may be so close to the surface that it causes a flexible liner to billow up from the bottom. This situation is known as 'hippoing' and although it can be remedied by covering the liner on the pool bottom with heavy slabs or stones, it is better to avoid the lowest point on such sites. The depth of the ground water can be checked by digging out a hole to about 60cm (2ft) deep, covering it and leaving for at least 24 hours. The water will seep in from the sides and settle to the depth of the water table.

◆ *Is electricity for a pump or lighting going to be accessible?*
Check on the shortest feasible route from your planned water feature to the nearest electrical source in your house, garage or shed. If you are starting from scratch, with an unworked plot, the task of laying cable will, of course, be easier than if you have to negotiate ready-made paths and flower

beds. Few problems are insurmountable, but long stretches of armoured cable and chiselling a route across a concrete driveway (see page 34) will eat into your budget.

◆ *Might wind be a problem?*
Wind funnelling between houses or other solid features has a distinctly cooling effect on water and may spoil the spray pattern of a fountain; it may also disturb the water surface too much for waterlilies, which like still water. A draughty position is also not so pleasant to sit in.

With the questions of style, position and other requirements resolved, the practical work can begin!

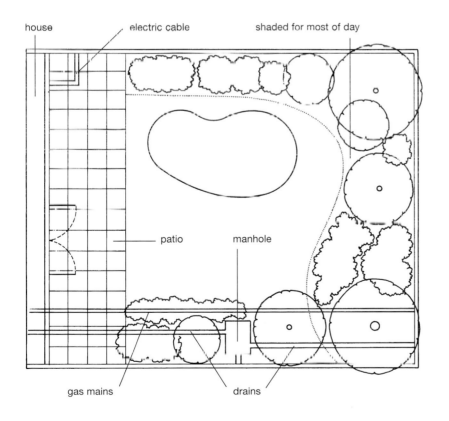

house   electric cable   shaded for most of day

patio   manhole

gas mains   drains

Before you begin to excavate, identify the position of the drains and gas mains and, if necessary, the electricity supply. Also, note how shadows fall across the garden at different times of the day so that the pool can be sited accordingly.

PRACTICALITIES

Whatever the style, size and shape of your water feature, the underlying construction and installation of it will follow a limited number of methods.

A pool, for instance, is simply a waterproof basin. It might be lined with clay or with concrete but the two simplest methods for a small pool are to use a pre-formed rigid liner or a flexible sheet liner.

Excavation

When digging out even a small pool, the amount of soil excavated is surprisingly large. Because the soil is not compressed as it was before, the spoil heap can look quite frightening – about twice the size of the hole. You will need to decide how to dispose of it all. If you are redesigning other parts of the garden, take this additional soil into account, perhaps in creating contouring, terracing or raised beds. Remember to keep the more fertile, cultivable topsoil – roughly the top 30cm (1ft) or so – separate from the denser subsoil. The subsoil is not suitable for growing purposes, but can obviously be used at the bottom of any newly created levels. If reshaping is not part of your plan, some topsoil can be redistributed over any beds or borders in the garden, but should be no deeper than about an extra 7–10cm (3–4in). The subsoil will have to be bagged up or emptied into a skip and disposed of.

PRE-FORMED LINERS

Rigid, pre-formed units are widely available in a variety of sizes and styles and most include one or more marginal shelves. It is best to choose a neutral colour that will blend in and not be obtrusive if any part shows above the water line.

Installing a pre-formed unit

1. For symmetrical or regular shapes like squares, rectangles or circles, place the unit upside down on the ground in the position it will occupy. Indicate the outline of the rim with sand or mark the soil with a spade. For an irregularly shaped unit, stand it upright in position, propping it up temporarily with bricks or blocks. Transfer the shape of the outline to the ground by inserting upright bamboo canes from the rim into the soil below in sufficient numbers for the outline to be clearly visible when the unit is removed. Use sand, string, or the edge of a spade to mark the outline in the soil.

2. As pre-formed pool units incorporate a marginal shelf, measure the depth of this shelf from the top of the unit and dig out a hole to this depth from 4in (10cm) outside the outline of the pool.

3. Identify the area to be dug out for the deeper zone of the pool unit by raking over the surface of the freshly dug hole and placing the unit back in the hole so that when pressed against the soft soil an imprint will be made to act as a guide.

4. Dig out this deeper zone to 5cm (2in) deeper than the maximum depth of the unit. This can be checked by measuring down to the bottom of the hole from a straight-edged piece of timber which straddles the sides of the excavation. Cover the bottom with 5cm (2in) of sand and smooth over the sides and shelves, removing any stones.

5. Place the unit back in the hole, pressing down gently and checking that the top is level all round with a spirit level on the straight edge of timber resting on opposite sides of the rim. Correct any discrepancies in level by removing the unit and adjusting the sand layer on the bottom. Once satisfied that it is entirely level, pour 10cm (4in) of water into the unit to keep it more stable.

6. Backfill the gap between the unit and the sides of the hole with sand or sifted soil, adding more water inside as backfilling proceeds. Keep checking that the unit remains level throughout the backfilling process until sufficient water is contained to keep the unit from moving.

A symmetrically shaped pre-formed pool should be inverted on the ground and the shape marked with sand or a spade. Stand the pool, the right way up, in the defined area to mark the dimensions of the deepest section.

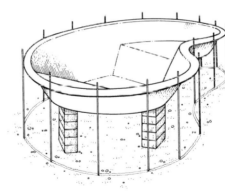

Support an asymmetrically shaped pool on bricks and insert bamboo canes vertically around the edge. Use sand or string to mark the outline of the pool.

Check that the pool is level with a spirit level. Rest a plank on opposite edges of the pool in several directions and add more sand under the pool until it is perfectly level.

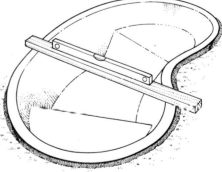

FLEXIBLE LINERS

Flexible liners are a much cheaper method of making pools than pre-formed units. They also allow greater versatillility in shape, particularly for informal pools, as the liner will follow whatever the shape of the excavation, rather than the hole having to be taken out to the pre-determined shape of a rigid liner. Their greatest advantage is in the construction of informal pools, where, by the effective shaping of the surroundings, informal beds of waterside planting are easier to construct.

Flexible liners are available in several materials and thicknesses, from polythene at the lower end of the price scale to butyl, which is the most expensive. The price range reflects their expected longevity – a flexible liner will eventually be weakened by the ultra-violet rays in natural light. As a guide, check the guarantee which gives a clue to the quality of the product. Black is the best colour for pools; it is the least obtrusive and gives a greater illusion of depth.

Measuring for liners

The size of liner required is calculated by adding twice the pool's depth to the maximum length and width, plus a bit extra as an allowance. So the calculation for a pool measuring 3 x 2m and 60cm deep (10 x 6 x 2ft) would be:

Metric			*Imperial*		
60cm x 2 =	1.2m		2ft x 2 =	4ft	
+ length	3m		+ length	9ft	
+ allowance	30cm		+ allowance	1ft	
=	4.5m length		=	14ft length	
60cm x 2 =	1.2m		2ft x 2 =	4ft	
+ width	2m		+ width	6ft	
+ allowance	30cm		+ allowance	1ft	
=	3.5m width		=	11ft width	

Installing a flexible liner

1. Mark out the outline of the pool with hosepipe, string or canes, then inscribe the outline with sand or a spade.

2. Insert pegs 15–22cm (6–9in) long, and approximately 2–3cm (1in) in diameter around the outline at intervals of 2m (6ft), leaving 5–7cm (2–3in) of the peg above the soil surface. On steeply sloping sites the pegs will need to be much longer.

3. Decide which of the pegs is going to be the benchmark for the final level of the pool and tap this peg in to the desired height. This will be called the datum peg.

4. With a straight-edged piece of timber longer than 2m (6ft), (the distance between the pegs), and a spirit level held on top of the straight edge, knock the adjacent peg in to the same height as the datum peg.

5. Go around the outline of the pool repeating step 4 until all the outline pegs are the same height as the datum peg. The pegs now give an accurate measure of how the ground fluctuates in level around the proposed pool so that you can carry out any necessary cutting or filling to achieve a level surround.

6. Start digging out the whole pool area from 5–7cm (2–3in) inside the outline to a depth of 22cm (9in). If digging out on grass, strip off the turf and stack the turves upside down in a convenient area to rot down. After 6–9 months this makes good loam for use in aquatic containers when potting on vigorous plants. When digging around the outside edge, make the edge at a slight angle to the vertical which helps to prevent the sides from crumbling away.

7. Mark out another inner outline for the deeper zone of the pool. Start this about 30cm (12in) inside the main pool outline to allow a marginal shelf all the way round the pool.

8. Dig out a further 37cm (15in) of soil from this deeper inner zone so that the final depth of the inner area of the pool is 60cm (2ft). Again, keep the edge of the deeper zone at a slight angle to the vertical.

9. Rake over the sides and bottom of the excavation to remove any sharp surfaces, then lay underlay in the hole, overlapping the edges of the rolls where required.

10. Drape the flexible liner into the hole loosely and temporarily secure around the edges with large stones or bricks. Ensure that there is adequate overlap around the sides so that as the weight of the water pressure pulls the liner into the hole there will still be adequate liner around the top.

11. Start filling the pool, teasing out any bad creases in the liner before the weight of the water makes this difficult.

12. As the water reaches its final level, minor corrections can be made with the small flap of surplus liner. The original level pegs can now be removed and the pool finished with whatever style of edging is required.

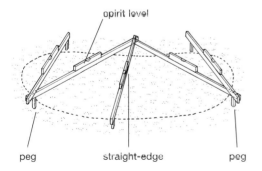

Drive pegs into the ground around the proposed edge of the pool, then check that the tops of the pegs are level with a straight-edge and spirit level.

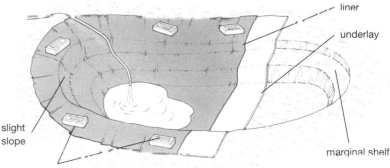

When you lay the liner make sure there is a generous margin around the edges because the weight of water will cause the liner to settle in the hole. Use bricks to hold the liner in position until the pond is full.

Some plants do best if their roots are in soil which never dries out. These bog or marginal plants include some of the finest foliage plants, including Hosta fortunei *var.* 'Albopicta' *and* H. f. *var.* 'Aureomarginata', Euphorbia griffithii 'Dixter', Corydalis flexuosa *and variegated irises.*

Liners are sold extensively by mail order or in aquatic centres and are readily available. There is an advantage in digging out and shaping the hole before purchasing the liner as you are then free to make adjustments to the shape as the excavation proceeds.

Flexible liners are usually used in conjunction with an underlay to protect the liner from any sharp edges in the hole. While old carpet is often used for this purpose, it will eventually rot, leaving the liner unprotected. Sand is also often recommended, but it can be easily dislodged from the sides of the hole when inserting the liner. Proprietary underlay of polyester matting sold in rolls 2m (6ft) wide is far better and lasts indefinitely.

MAKING A BOG GARDEN

A bog garden beside a pool can be constructed simply by extending the liner beyond the pool's perimeter on one side to form a saucer-shaped bed about 30–37cm (12–15in) deep which is then filled with soil. In order to prevent this soil from becoming waterlogged and sour, use a fork to pierce small drainage holes about 1m (3ft) apart in the liner. This allows slow drainage but sufficient moisture retention for the bog plants provided the soil used in the beds is heavy or adequately enriched with organic matter. With this method ensure that the pool sides are high enough to prevent the pool water seeping into the bed or you will need to keep topping up the pool.

A bog garden does not have to be adjacent to a pool and it is quite easy to build one as an independent feature. The method is simplicity itself, requiring no more than a sheet of old polythene. Dig a hole of whatever size or shape you require, excavating to a depth of 30–37cm

(12–15in). Line the hole with polythene or pool liner and puncture with a fork, as above. To prevent the holes clogging with soil, sprinkle pea gravel over the holes before refilling the bed with good-quality heavy soil, preferably with as much well-rotted organic matter added as possible. Cut off any surplus liner which remains exposed when the bed is filled and hide the edge of the liner by folding it back under the soil. Although the bed will need watering periodically in very dry weather, this simple construction prevents the soil from drying out as quickly as it would otherwise.

CONSTRUCTING A RAISED POOL

Raised pools save having to dig holes and cart away soil which can be a problem in terraced houses. They are particularly attractive to the elderly, allowing the water to be touched more easily and the detail of plants and fish to be seen at close quarters.

They are, however, more prone to freezing in cold areas and if not deep enough may prove unsuitable to overwinter fish. Adequate precautions should be taken against damage to the pool walls by expansion of ice in prolonged severe frost (see page 46).

One of the easiest ways of making a raised pool is to use a rigid liner and surround it with a material of your choice. Walling stones or bricks are the most permanent but are normally the most costly and, if mortared, require skill in bricklaying. There are several cheaper and simpler alternatives, such as log rolls which require little skill or time. Sink the rigid unit partly into the ground, leaving the marginal shelf region above ground level. Rake the area where the deep zone of the pool will be positioned and dig out just sufficient depth to bring the pool rim, when in position, to the same height above the ground as the height of the log roll. Firm the unit into position and unwrap the log roll around the pool, securing it in place by nailing the roll to wooden posts which have been firmed into the ground at 1m (3ft) intervals. Fill any gaps between the logs and the pool

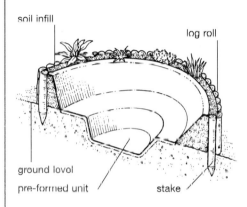

soil infill
log roll
ground level
pre-formed unit
stake

A partially raised pool can be made from a rigid, pre-formed unit and log roll, which is simply attached to stakes inserted around the pool.

Waterfall and stream constructions allow you to create shallow rock pools that will hold water and so sustain interest when the waterfall is not running. Still rock pools combined with an element of flowing water are typical of the best and most attractive sort of small water feature.

rim with soil and plant small spreading plants to soften the edges and hide the rim.

If you would like the effect of a mortared stone wall, there are modular wall blocks which are manufactured to appear like smaller blocks mortared together. They are secured on top of each other by using a proprietary fixative, and are usually straightforward to assemble but some look more realistic than others.

Further variations include making dry stone walls or sloping rock banks around the raised pool, which will provide an ideal home for alpines.

If you have, or can provide, bricklaying skills, then a very satisfactory pool can be made from a double wall of bricks or walling blocks with a flexible liner laid across the bottom and sandwiched between the inner and outer side walls. If using blocks rather than bricks, you will need to render the outside to make it more attractive. This is the method used for the Raised Pool on pages 58–9.

ADDING MOVING WATER
Streams and waterfalls

On a sloping site it is very tempting to introduce a small stream and waterfall with the aid of a recirculating pump. A simple stream can be made with rocks and flexible liner, in the same way as an informal pool. Construction has been made very easy by the availability of a wide range of pre-formed stream units in fibreglass or plastic. Choose carefully from the various finishes – some, once installed and disguised with planting, contribute a realistic rock effect; others will forever look moulded.

One of the charms of a small stream is that it gives you the opportunity to create small shallow rock pools which remain filled with water when the pump is turned off. These rock pools attract a variety of birds to drink and bathe and make an additional bonus to the movement and sound of a stream. Pre-formed stream units that incorporate rock pools are worth the extra investment in making the stream look more natural when the pump is not operating.

Installation of pre-formed units is not difficult. Working from the bottom upwards, lay the units so that the outlet of the one above provides ample overlap for the water to spill. The stream units are designed so that even when laid level the rock pools will hold water and at the same time spill over into the pool below. The origin of the stream usually takes the form of a small but deeper rock pool which is called the header pool; like the smaller rock pools lower down, it retains water when the pump is turned off.

The water circulates by means of a submersible pump sited in the base pool, which delivers water through a flexible pipe to the header pool at the top of the watercourse. The pipe is buried in the soil alongside the stream after the units or the rocks and liner have been installed. The point at which this pipe discharges the water into the header pool is normally disguised with small rocks. This is also a useful point to hide a flow-adjusting valve. Once all the installation is complete, very little liner will be visible below the rocks, but the edges of stream units can be disguised by carpeting alpines such as arabis, aubrieta, alpine phlox and alyssum.

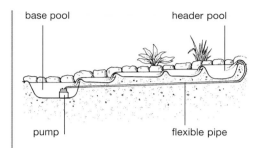

Pre-formed stream units are relatively simple to install. Remember to work from the bottom up.

Fountains

In addition to providing interest through movement and sound, fountains have a very useful function in the hot weather if you have fish in your pool. Adequately stocked with submerged plants, the oxygen levels in the water during the daytime are supplemented by pure oxygen given off through the leaves in a process called photosynthesis. Most of the oxygen in a pool is absorbed from the water surface, and the warmer the weather, the less able the water is to absorb oxygen from the air. During the night the submerged plants reverse their role in providing oxygen, requiring oxygen themselves and giving off carbon dioxide. This condition can cause real stress to fish,

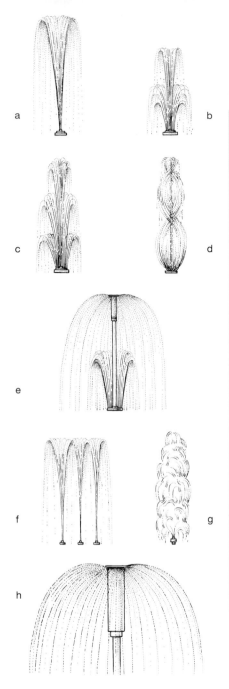

A variety of fountain effects: a simple spray (a); multi-tier effects: a two-tiered spray (b) and a three-tiered spray (c); novelty effects: a whirling spray (d) and a Tiffany jet (e); jets: a surface jet (f) and a bubbling geyser (g); and a bell jet (h).

particularly on warm nights and if the stocking levels of fish are high. In these conditions a fountain with a fine spray pattern can be lifesaving if left on during the night. The fine droplets of water pick up vital oxygen which is re-absorbed into the pond water as the droplets splash back on the surface and there is increased turbulence.

When choosing a fountain the basic choice lies between two main groups: those which spray water into the air through a variety of nozzle sizes and types, and the free-standing ornamental wall fountains which spout or send cascades of water into shallow basins below. There are now several variations of both types, particularly for small water features such as self-contained wall fountains, cobble fountains, millstone fountains, geysers and brimming urns.

In order to make the installation of a spray fountain a relatively easy exercise, many submersible pump kits include the fittings to install a simple spray fountain. These comprise a plastic spray nozzle, a short length of rigid pipe to extend the nozzle above the water line, a flow adjustor and a T-piece to allow a small waterfall to be added if required. These are simplicity itself to assemble and can be adequate for a small pool, providing the type of spray pattern which oxygenates the water. A visit to a good aquatic centre will illustrate the much wider variety of spray patterns possible to achieve. Follow these basic guidelines when making a choice:

◆ Ensure that the fountain pump is adequate to do the job: a spray jet requires considerably more pressure than a water spout simply delivering water from the same height.

◆ Keep the height of sprays and jets of water to the scale of the pool. The more the height of the spray exceeds the diameter of the pool, the greater the risk of spray blowing over the sides and the fountain looking out of proportion.

◆ Where a fountain is to be seen from a distance, avoid too fine a spray jet which could be lost in a background of mixed foliage.

- Position a fountain with a delicate spray pattern towards the sun so that the spray will sparkle in the light. Keep the background simple and subdued.

- Fine fountain jets soon clog, particularly in areas of hard water. Ensure that the jets are accessible enough to be removed easily for regular cleaning and descaling.

- Fountains can be noisy. A flow-adjusting valve either on the pump or inserted in the piping will enable you to make an intrusive restless noise gentler and more soothing.

- If you are going to plant waterlilies, avoid fountains which cause too much turbulence over a large area of the pool surface. Waterlilies resent any form of current, water turbulence or regular wetting of their leaves with fountain droplets.

- In exposed situations wider jet nozzles are most appropriate in reducing water loss from wind spray. The geyser jet is particularly appropriate for windy sites, creating a wide mouth of frothy water. A stronger pump is necessary for these jets as they depend on air being drawn in through small holes in the sides of the fountain jet.

PUMPS AND ELECTRICITY

As small water features become more popular, electrical products to make their effect more innovative through movement and lighting have become more widely available. In a small garden the cost of extending the electricity to a water feature need not be prohibitive and the technical advances made in the manufacture of submersible pumps have made the running costs negligible.

Connecting up

The first decision in considering a pump or lighting for a water feature will be whether it is to be mains or low voltage. In a low voltage system, the

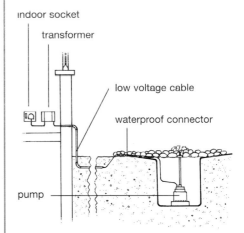

For a low voltage system, the cable is taken from the house to the pond, with a transformer used to reduce the supply from the mains.

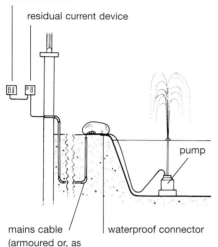

indoor socket

residual current device

pump

mains cable
(armoured or, as
here, in a conduit)

waterproof connector

A mains voltage cable fitted with a contact circuit breaker (residual current device) instantly cuts off the supply in case of accidents.

mains supply is reduced through a transformer, normally sited indoors close to the mains socket. As there is a very natural concern at the mix of water and electricity, many pool owners prefer the reassurance of a low voltage supply in the event of a short circuit or cable break, although this anxiety has been largely overcome by the advent of contact circuit breakers (residual current devices or RCDs). These are fitted as standard on all outdoor electrical sockets and are capable of cutting off the electricity supply instantly in the event of damage or a short circuit. Low voltage pumps are limited in their choice and output and in many situations it will be necessary to use mains voltage where the range is almost overwhelming.

It is vital that all fittings are installed by a qualified electrician and that connectors, switches and sockets are approved for outdoor use. Cabling for mains voltage should either be armoured cable or protected by suitable conduit. Before connecting up, however, you will need to prepare the route for the cabling from the nearest electrical connection to the site. Mains cable will need to be buried at least 45cm (18in) deep under lawn or flower beds, and any paving *en route* will have to be lifted and the cable laid below it. If there is a stretch of concrete you cannot bypass, you will need to chisel out a channel for the conduit (thread the cable through before laying the conduit) and then concrete it over again. In planning you will need to balance the convenience of laying cable via an easy route, ideally one not regularly cultivated, and the additional cost of extra cable – armoured cable is expensive.

Once you have laid the cable, it is useful to mark the route on a plan of the garden, so that you have a reference should you be undertaking further work some time in the future.

If connecting up to the mains, even with low voltage cable, proves impractical, you may like to consider a more recent advance, the introduction of a solar-powered pump. This is, however, only powerful enough for a very small pump.

Pump choice

Small water features frequently require no more than a submersible pump which is supplied with an adequate length of sealed cable to reach a switch box or connector near the pool side. This is in turn connected by underground armoured cable to the mains socket outlet fitted with a contact circuit breaker. The size of the pump will relate to its role, either a fountain or a waterfall. In choosing the pump the supplier will need to know the answers to the following questions:

◆ What is the size and depth of the pool?

◆ Is the pump to operate a fountain or waterfall or a combination of the two?

◆ If a fountain, what is the height and type of spray?

◆ If a waterfall, what is the height and distance to the top of the watercourse from the pump, and the width of the waterfall?

◆ Will the pump be operating continuously or intermittently?

Armed with this information the supplier is in a much better position to recommend a suitable size and type of pump. If the pump is expected to operate continuously, it is advisable to check on the running costs. Some pumps are more efficient than others in this respect, and a small additional outlay can save a great deal later. Many water features such as wall fountains and small bubble fountains are supplied as a kit, complete with pump.

When specifying fittings to the electrician, it is a useful tip to instal a two-way or three-way switch-box even though only one switch may be required. This way any later additional fittings such as a spotlight or filter can be installed more easily. Standard garden hosepipe, which is approximately 13mm (½in) in diameter, will fit the outlet of most pumps, but cheap hosepipe can perish quickly and become quite brittle. Reinforced, black flexible

A submersible pump such as the one shown here would be suitable for most small fountains and streams.

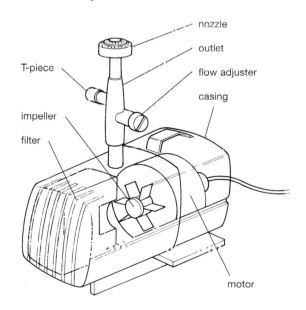

nozzle
outlet
flow adjuster
casing
T-piece
impeller
filter
motor

Suffused lighting and carefully positioned foliage add a special dimension to this wall-mounted fountain feature.

piping is more suitable and it is available at most water garden suppliers. A useful additional purchase is a flow adjustor, an adjustable valve inserted into the pipe at a convenient point that enables you to control the rate of flow from the pump.

Lighting

Like pumps, there are two basic types of lighting: low voltage and mains voltage, with the same safety rules applicable to their installation. If the lighting is to be seen from any distance in the garden, it will probably be necessary to use mains voltage – low voltage lamps are only suitable for small schemes viewed at close quarters as the illumination levels are very low.

All lighting designed for underwater installation comes as a sealed unit. Since these can get very hot they must always be underwater when switched on, to keep the lens cool. Lights on a low voltage system are not so crucial in this respect as the light levels are so much lower.

Once you are happy that the lighting is giving just the effect you want, conceal land-based units as much as possible under plants or behind rocks, so that their casings are unobtrusive.

FINISHING TOUCHES

The success or failure of a water feature is greatly influenced by the quality and finish of the edging. This is particularly relevant to small water features where a poor finish to the surrounds, either in the choice of material or in the quality of construction, will be much more noticeable than in a larger pool where the fine detail is more easily lost.

Formal water features need crisp, strong edges and the surround must be

level when mirrored in the water when any variance from parallel lines would be noticed immediately. Informal pools may be less demanding in this respect but less attention to detail may mean exposed liner at the edge, an equally irritating weakness as there should be no sign of the liner in a well-constructed pool. Whereas a formal pool will have the total perimeter of hard edging, an informal pool can have a mixture of surfaces ranging from grass and plants to crazy paving, paving slabs, rocks, cobbles and timber.

PAVING SLABS

Although York stone slabs have a natural texture and colour, they are expensive, prone to attracting algae and can become slippery. This is particularly noticeable in reclaimed slabs which have worn smooth after years of use in pavements. Reclaimed slabs also tend to vary in thickness, making it difficult to achieve the formality of parallel lines at the water's edge.

RECONSTITUTED AND CONCRETE PAVING SLABS

These are available in a wide range of shades and textures and each slab has an identical thickness. Those with a riven finish look well near water and several types have a roughened surface to prevent slipping. Slabs come in a number of standard sizes, including wedge shapes. When planning your pool size, you can save yourself a lot of trouble if you tailor its dimensions to avoid having to cut these heavy slabs.

When laying slabs, ensure that they are mortared on to a firm foundation to prevent any movement, and lay the slabs slightly overlapping the water.

A simple pool is made into something special by the use of widely varying hard landscaping materials: pavers, pebbles and stone blocks are all carefully placed to create fascinating, eye-catching patterns.

A variety of materials is suitable for the hard edging of a formal pool. Whichever material is selected, the pool liner should never be visible.

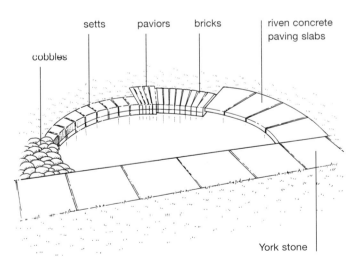

cobbles · setts · paviors · bricks · riven concrete paving slabs · York stone

BRICKS

Bricks are excellent for small formal pools, being adaptable to a variety of shapes including circles. They should be laid at right angles to the water and not parallel. Ensure that the bricks are well baked and waterproof in order to resist frost damage when wet. Engineering bricks are particularly suitable as they are extremely hard-wearing and waterproof.

BRICK PAVIORS

Similar in appearance and size to bricks but made with concrete rather than clay, paviors are harder-wearing and more resistant to frost damage. In addition to a selection of colours, some are available with a rounded edge which forms an attractive detail on a circular pool edge.

SETTS

Setts are available in granite, sandstone and concrete and are generally cube-shaped between 10 and 20cm (4–8in) square. Like bricks and paviors they are ideal for edging small formal pools, providing a very distinctive finish.

COBBLES

Round beach cobbles make a very attractive surround, particularly if they vary in size to give a more natural effect, grading from small to large as one climbs away from the water. Ensure that the cobbles are washed thoroughly in case of any salt residue.

Some gravel quarries supply a cheaper grade of loose cobbles which have a high percentage of split cobbles present. These should be avoided if they are placed on top of liners as the edges are extremely sharp. Certain gravels and shingles also have piercingly sharp edges and should not be used too close to flexible liners. You should always check with a sample first if in doubt over sharp edges.

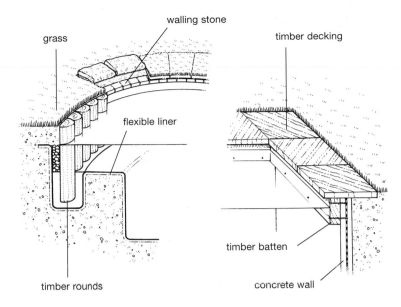

grass

walling stone

timber decking

flexible liner

timber rounds

timber batten

concrete wall

TIMBER

Pool surrounds in various forms of timber are becoming increasingly popular, particularly timber decking in either decking tiles or planks. Decking not only gives a clean edge, but can be used to provide a large overlap, giving the illusion that it bridges the water or forms a jetty. Rounds of timber placed side by side or proprietary log roll are very useful when a pool is edged by grass in preventing the grass from crumbling or sinking with heavy wear. The tops of the timbers should be kept just below the level of the grass in order to keep a clean mowing edge.

GRASS

Despite the risk of grass mowings flying in the water and bare patches through heavy wear, grass looks natural and forms a restful and inviting edge in informal pools. A good method to prevent the grass from sinking and growing in the water is to form a small strong foundation of natural walling stone underneath the turf and below the water line at the edge.

PLANTED SURROUNDS

There are many moisture loving herbaceous plants and shrubs which can form informal edges to the water and are particularly suitable around a wildlife pool to give extra cover. These plants are not marginal plants which require their roots to be grown in saturated soil, but plants which thrive in moist but not waterlogged soil. Such plants are often supplied in catalogues or plant centres as bog plants. Around a natural pond these plants will flourish around the sides, drawing the moisture they need from the soil water and the pond. See the suggestions for plants on pages 122–6.

An informal pool will look more attractive with a timber or grass edging. Grass will need to be supported on a stone wall or timber rounds if it is not eventually to sink into the water.

MAINTENANCE

A pond is the primary focus of this courtyard garden, and it has been carefully planted to sustain its health and beauty. Water gardening doesn't just happen in the water – pool edges and surrounds will provide some wonderful opportunities for keen gardeners.

A well-planted pool which has achieved the right balance between plants and water, providing glimpses of a submerged world, is still one of the greatest attractions of water in the garden, but all too often the result is a disappointment: green, cloudy and overgrown.

Green water

Expose any shallow quantity of water to daylight and the water soon becomes green, and the problem most frequently encountered in maintaining small water features is green water. Various aquatic plants and time for the water to find its own balance will combat this natural phenomenon in open water. As an alternative or a supplement to clear the water, various methods of filtration can be introduced to reduce algae, notably ultra-violet filters which rely on the pool water passing over a concentrated ultra-violet light source. This is necessary in small reflecting pools such as the one on pages 74–5, where plants would break the severity and simplicity of the design.

If daylight is excluded from the main body of water (for instance, in a reservoir below a millstone fountain), the offending algae which green the water cannot survive. These 'closed' systems, which circulate water from light-excluded reservoirs, have become increasingly popular through their lack of maintenance and increasingly innovative designs.

Also available are proprietary solutions which have been specially formulated for adding to small water features like barrels and self-contained fountains where problems of smell and bacteria can build up because of their small water volume.

Cloudy water

Cloudy water is the result of minute algae thriving on light and mineral salts. As fresh tap water is charged with mineral salts and there is also little shade from light in most new pools, algae quickly develop and there is little to be done until the plants start to grow.

Two important types of plant required for a pool are submerged plants, often referred to as oxygenators, and plants with surface leaves such as waterlilies to provide shade. When making a new pool it is important to plant these two types of plant as soon as possible, particularly the waterlilies, as it takes a number of weeks before there are sufficient leaves to be effective in reducing light. During this initial period the pool would benefit from scattering floating plants on the surface to provide shade. The most common hardy floating plant is duckweed (*Lemna*) and although this should not be introduced to large pools where it can get out of control and be difficult to remove, it is relatively easy to remove with a net on small pools. A less hardy and slightly less invasive floater is fairy moss (*Azolla*) which is an extremely attractive little fern which turns pleasant shades of orange in the autumn before sinking to the bottom. As the waterlilies become established these floaters can be netted off. Meanwhile the other submerged plants, the oxygenators, will be competing with the algae for the dissolved mineral salts. This role of starving out the algae is more important to the healthy balance in the pond than their ability to produce underwater oxygen, a function which is only performed in daylight.

At all costs resist the temptation to change the water in this initial period of cloudiness. It is only temporary and any new water introduced from the tap will cloud over in the same way. Be patient and one morning there will be the most pleasant surprise, the pool will have suddenly cleared.

Pests such as greenfly can be removed from the foliage of water plants by directing a strong jet of water on to the leaves.

Other pool problems

Apart from the problem of algae, aquatic plants are relatively free of pests and diseases that are likely to kill, rather than just weaken the plant. Most pests, like greenfly, can be dealt with by giving the foliage a strong jet of water or dunking it for a few hours when the aphids will either be drowned or eaten by fish. The nature of water gardening precludes the use of insecticides which could pollute the water, and pest and disease control lies mainly in maintaining good hygiene rather than in chemical cures. The main disfiguring pests occur on the leaves of waterlilies and regular removal of older or infected leaves goes a long way to keep such pests at bay.

One threat to which you might think a small pool immune endangers not the plant life, but fish: the heron. Many gardeners who believed their modest pool beneath a heron's interest have been astonished to find it cleaned out by one of these elegant but predatory birds. Talk to neighbours to discover if heron are a problem. Everyone has a favourite deterrent, from decoys and heron scarers to an overhead network of fishing line to prevent the bird landing. Heron do not swoop down on fish like a fish eagle or a pelican, but wade in from the side, so a double strand of thread or wire around the pool about 45–60cm (18–24in) high is usually effective. As a precautionary measure, provide your fish with plenty of cover, in the form of surface leaves and, in the deeper zone, a couple of lengths of pipe in which they can hide (drain pipes are good for this).

ROUND-THE-YEAR CARE
Spring

If the old foliage on marginal plants was left on for the winter, it can now be cut back as the weather warms up and the danger of serious frost passes, taking care not to cut into the young green growth. If the plants are starting to outgrow their containers, the plant should be removed and divided (see propagation methods on pages 49–51).

Clean off any algae that have developed on paving at the poolside and check over the structure of pool walls for signs of any damage that prolonged frost may have caused and make any necessary repairs.

Pumps can be reinstalled or lowered back on to the pool bottom if they have been running throughout the winter.

Consider any new planting which will improve the design from the previous year.

As the days get warmer, a filamentous form of alga causes the growth of a mass of dense strands known as blanketweed which frequently occurs in otherwise completely clear water. The blanketweed tends to cling to plants and containers, and in some cases becomes so thick and extensive that it can trap small fish. It is particularly prevalent in early spring when light levels are high but before the leaves have grown to help shade the surface. In small pools it can be removed by hand with a forked stick or rake and this process may have to be repeated as soon as it gains hold again.

Blanketweed can be removed with a forked stick.

Summer

The major maintenace task in the summer is to maintain a healthy balance between plants and water so that algae do not get out of hand. Regularly remove faded foliage and thin out overcrowded plants. This is particularly important in small naturalistic pools where water perennials, if left unthinned and tended, would gradually turn the pool into a boggy little marsh. Too few plants, however, and there could be a surge of algae growth in periods of hot sunny weather and the pool could become cloudy. A visit to aquatic centres to see the range of algicides on display is a clue to how common this problem is.

The water level will probably need topping up from time to time and if large quantities of tap water are added frequently, the fine water balance can be lost and two forms of algae, the small single-celled algae responsible for clouding the water and a more filamentous algae that cause blanketweed, capitalize on the injection of mineral salts. Chemicals can be used but their effectiveness is weakened where they have to act without killing other desirable plants or weaken fish. In a pool without fish and plants a filtration system or the use of aquatic weedkillers will almost guarantee a clear pond.

A heavily stocked pool, on the other hand, is a difficult environment for algicides to work in and results from their use are varied. Inevitably it tends to be a slow process in achieving control and chemicals known as pH adjustors or balancers are the most benign but effective with time. Their action is to reduce the alkalinity of the water to levels that are less favourable to algae and they have achieved more success than many algicides. If the pool is topped up with alkaline water, the pool-balancing chemical will have to be used more frequently, so one answer is to use collected rainwater. This is generally acid and much less likely to upset the balance. In dry areas where the pool is less likely to receive much natural topping up, diverting water through rainwater barrels by connecting a hose from the tap to the pool makes use of every drop of water going. This may lead to too much at one time in heavy rainstorms, so you will need to be able to divert the system to prevent the pool overflowing in prolonged downpours.

Waterlily leaves are being constantly replaced in the summer and, as they age, they have a tendency to go yellow, which not only looks unsightly but eventually adds decaying plant debris to the water. Keep removing the yellowing or dead leaves and dead flowers – the result can be quite a transformation of a rather tired-looking pool to a much healthier and more attractive feature. The same routine of removing dead or decaying foliage should be applied to all the plants, marginals included. If the waterlilies are

If you need to top up the pond, rainwater is usually better than tap water, which is usually too alkaline. Collect rainwater in a butt and connect a hose to the tap at the base of the butt.

looking tired they may be starved in the containers after a year. Feed them with proprietary tablets or sachets of slow-release fertilizers.

If a pump is installed, keep checking the strainer which can clog up with debris and algae quite quickly, considerably reducing its performance. Similarly, the jets on any fountains need regular cleaning. In hot weather, keep the fountain or waterfall on at night to help supply fish with oxygen.

As the summer progresses it is a good time to consider the periodic clean-out which should take place every three to four years, depending on how well the pool has been maintained and the amount of fish and submerged plantlife. See pages 47–8 for details.

A balanced planting of marginals, floating and submerged plants will maintain the health of the water and the fish you may wish to introduce to a water garden.

Autumn

The submerged plants will have grown exten-sively during the summer and now is the best time to cut them hard back before the winter. The plants will die back and rot in the winter months and the decaying stems and leaves will accumulate on the pool bottom causing a build-up of detritus, the evil-smelling black mulm which is familiar to anyone who has cleaned out a pond. The remaining waterlily leaves and flowers should also be removed before they die completely and join any rotting matter on the bottom. If you have many deciduous trees and shrubs around the garden, spread a net over the pool to prevent leaves from falling into the water and rotting. A short vertical net like a wire fence around the perimeter of the pool can be as valuable as a net over the surface, particularly in a windy

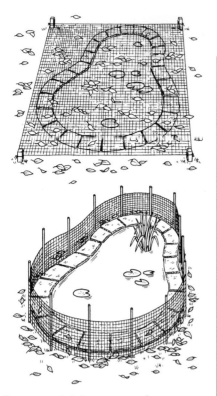

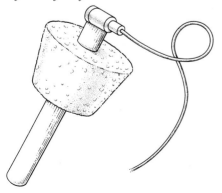

*In autumn it is important to keep
deciduous leaves out of the pool. The
easiest way is to stretch a net across the top
of the pool or, if leaves tend to be blown
across the garden, to erect a temporary low
fence of wire around the pool.*

*A floating heater will keep a small area
of water free of ice in the coldest weather.*

area where the leaves are blown rather than fall directly into the water. The foliage on marginal plants will turn a straw colour but tend to remain on the plants rather than fall into the water. The tidy-minded gardener may prefer to remove this foliage now and in so doing remove the refuge of overwintering pests. But in gardens exposed to the cold winds of early spring this old foliage provides some protection to the emerging young growth, and in a wildlife garden not only looks more natural but will give extra cover to amphibians emerging from hibernation in spring.

Winter

Keeping a variety of foliage and flower throughout the year is not easy with a small area of water, as most aquatic plants die down in the winter and any foliage left tends to be straw-coloured. It can help to incorporate the pool planting into its surroundings (which might include evergreens or winter-interest plants). Winter is one of the best times to enjoy reflections on the water surface, after the waterlilies have died down, and coloured stems and outlines of plants become highlighted in the water.

If they are not going to be used over the winter, pumps, filters and lighting should be removed, cleaned and stored. If you intend to continue using the pump it should be placed on a plinth so that it pumps from shallower water. The reason for doing this is to prevent the pump from mixing the warmer water which sinks to the bottom in winter with the colder water near the surface.

When the pump is removed, the electric connection can be used to allow a floating pool heater to be installed. This prevents a small area of the water surface from freezing and is invaluable in making life easier for fish and in avoiding the danger of expanding ice damaging the side walls of the pool. A further advantage of preventing a solid sheet of ice from persisting too long is that the unfrozen area allows the escape of harmful gases like methane from under the ice. If methane, which is caused by organic matter decaying in the water, is not allowed to escape, but is re-absorbed into the water, it can be toxic to fish. If it is not possible to use an electric pool heater, the expansion problem can be alleviated by floating rubber balls or pieces of polystyrene foam on the surface to absorb the pressure. Holes in the ice to float these objects can be made by standing a hot pan on the ice until it melts. Never break the ice with a hammer as the vibrations can traumatize torpid fish underneath. If there is a cover of snow on top of the ice, remove this as it tends to insulate the ice against melting more quickly in a thaw and denies light to submerged life.

THE POND CLEAN-OUT

From time to time the pond will need a thorough clean-out where the plants are removed and the silt removed from the bottom of the pond. Depending on the size of the pool, the density of planting and whether there are fish to take into account, this operation should be carried out approximately every three to four years. The timing of the operation is quite important as the disturbance to the many inhabitants of a pool should be kept to a minimum, and plants need to be able to recover and start growing again quickly. Mid to late summer is therefore a good time as there are no creatures in hibernation and plants can become re-established quickly. An overcast day is ideal as plants such as the waterlilies will quickly wilt in strong sunshine.

Waders and rubber gloves with long waterproof sleeves will prove invaluable even in relatively small ponds. Have ready a collection of large buckets (empty plastic dustbins are even better) distributed around the pond in readiness for holding submerged plants and underwater creatures. Newspapers are also useful when soaked to cover the foliage of waterlilies in sunny weather.

The first consideration will be to catch any fish with the minimum of trauma to them. If they are regularly fed in one place, begin by placing as

hose leading to drain

Ponds need to be cleaned out from time to time. The aim is to disrupt as little as possible the plants and any fish and animal life in the pond, which should be transferred to temporary containers. Use a hose to drain away the water so that you can get to the floor of the pool.

large a net as possible underneath the feeding zone and providing a small feed. Once netting out starts they become very wary and much more difficult to find. Remove as many as possible before the water becomes cloudy through the turbulence of the catch. A paddling pool makes a good temporary home during the clean-out, filled with water from the pool to minimize changes. Keep the temporary tank in the shade and spray over the water surface with a fine hose every hour or so throughout the day to help increase the oxygen content of the water.

Start removing water from the pool, by siphoning out if there is a lower point for the outlet. If a submersible pump is installed, this can be used to pump out by disconnecting the outlet from the waterfall or fountain pipe and attaching instead a length of garden hose which leads to a drain or a lower point away from the pool. On very small features baling out may be all that is necessary.

Fill all the available watertight containers around the pool with the pool water. This water contains numerous micro-organisms which should be reintroduced to the pool after the clean-out.

As the water level gets lower, the plants in the containers around the margins can be lifted out and stored nearby. They will not need immersing in shallow water unless the operation is delayed and the pool is empty for longer than a couple of days. Net off any elusive fish which remain.

As soon as the water level is low enough, remove the containers on the pool bottom, wearing non-studded wellingtons if the pool is made with a flexible liner. If the containers are large seek help to lift them, as saturated soil is extremely heavy.

The point will be reached where it becomes difficult to siphon or pump the last of the muddy water, and this has to be baled out. Use a plastic dustpan and brush, never use a shovel or spade with a sharp thin edge in case this damages the bottom. With all of the bottom mud removed give a good rinse with the hose and wipe down the sides, baling out the rinsing water.

Check over the surface of the pool bottom and sides for any cracks or damage and repair these with the appropriate repair kit for the type of pond.

Before refilling it is a good opportunity to examine the waterlilies, oxygenators and other submerged plants to see if they should be propagated or repotted (see below).

Begin refilling as soon as possible if fish are being housed in temporary quarters and replace the bottom plants while placing is easier in the shallow water. There are proprietary treatments which can be added to tap water to reduce the stress caused to the fish by the rapid change into chlorinated water. There is not so much urgency with the marginals as these can generally be replaced from the pool sides. Replace some of the original pool water which has been stored during the cleaning operation so that the micro-organisms can soon begin to achieve a satisfactory biological balance again in the water. Like the deep-water plants, the marginals will benefit from repotting or dividing before replacing in the water.

It is perfectly natural for many of the waterlily leaves to die off after division or repotting. Remove these by cutting the leaf stalks low down with a sharp knife or scissors rather than leaving them to rot. As with the establishment of a new pool, this would be a good time to scatter floaters on the surface of the clean pool to help regain the balance in the water.

PROPAGATION

Aquatic plants grow very quickly and the vast majority can be propagated by the simplest method of all: dividing the roots. This method applies to most of the marginals and waterlilies, although the techniques for waterlilies vary, depending on the species involved. The second main method, softwood cuttings, is appropriate to the oxygenating plants with their long trailing stems. Propagation by seed is the most useful method for a few species but is usually less practical if you are unlikely to need the vast numbers of offspring this method produces.

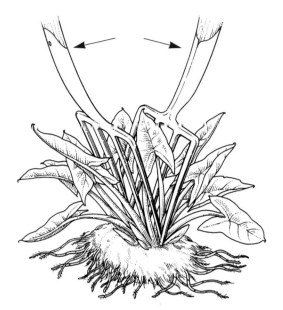

One of the easiest ways of dividing marginal plants is to place two forks, back to back, into the rootball.

Waterlilies can be propagated by removing the small protuberances from the tuber and inserting them in the growing medium.

remove for propagation

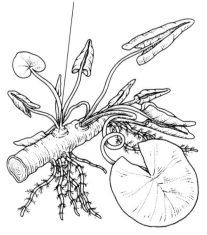

Division of marginal plants

This method is the same as for most herbaceous perennials and simply involves splitting the clumps of root into two or more portions. The problem with containerized aquatics is that if left too long in the containers, their roots become densely entangled with the mesh sides and the container may have to be sacrificed. Some roots are so thick that a spade may have to be used to sever the portions; this is particularly so with the thicker-rooted species which develop hard rhizomes. Discard the older pieces, normally in the centre of the clump, and select young vigorous portions to be potted up in aquatic baskets filled with aquatic compost to their original depth. The containers are then replaced on the marginal shelves in the pool; surplus plants can be held in shallow watertight containers with the water just covering the crowns.

Propagating waterlilies

Lift the plant and wash the roots thoroughly. Remove the old leaves and cut the plump root into sections 5–7cm (2–3in) long, each piece having young growth at its tip. Trim the young white thin roots under the thick rhizome right back almost to the main root, then press the prepared piece on to the firmed compost in an almost full medium-sized aquatic basket. Keep the growing tip above the surface at a slight upright angle, as it was growing originally, and topdress with pea shingle (do not cover the growing point). Immerse back in the pool on a pier of bricks so that there is no more than 5–7cm (2–3in) of water above the growing point. The container is gradually lowered as the young plant develops by removing layers of the supporting bricks under the aquatic basket.

Certain waterlilies have tuberous roots rather than longer rhizomes, and when lifted will show small protuberances on the tuber which can be snapped off by hand. These small growths can then be firmed on to the surface of aquatic compost in filled baskets and immersed like the more common waterlilies with rhizomes.

Softwood cuttings

These cuttings can be taken at any time during the summer as part of thinning and cutting back vigorous oxygenating plants under the water. It needs no special skill: simply nip or snip off the tops of the long stems to about 15–22cm (6–9in) long, and bunch 8 or 9 shoots together near the base with florists' wire. Insert the bunches into 10cm (4in) pots of aquatic compost, keeping the wire tie just under the compost. Totally immerse into watertight containers in a warm, partially shaded site where they should root in 2–3 weeks and can be transferred into larger baskets before planting in the pond.

Seed

Certain aquatics are difficult to propagate by division or cuttings and seed is the answer here. Collect the fresh seed as soon as it has ripened and scatter it evenly on a small seed pan filled with aquatic compost, covering the seed with 3mm (⅛in) of fine grit and water it with a fine rose. Place the pan in a washing-up bowl and gently introduce water into the bowl until it just covers the seed pan. Keep the water topped up to this level in a light, frost-free place where there is sunshine for part of the day. When the seedlings are large enough to handle prick them out into (7.5cm) 3in pots of aquatic compost and return to the watertight bowl. Seedlings of deep-water plants should be covered with 2–3cm (1in) of water and marginals kept in water at the same level as the top of the compost. When large enough the seedlings can be transferred into aquatic containers.

Fresh seed can be scattered over the surface of the growing medium and the container placed in a bowl and just covered with water.

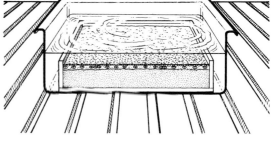

FORMAL POOLS

In small formal gardens the hard landscaping of terraces and pathways often forms the main theme in the design, and a pool can help to break the monotony of the uniform stone surfaces and serve as a link between natural plant forms and the constructed environment.

A formal garden design is one in which all the component parts combine symmetrically around a linear plan. Paths and borders are arranged along a main axis leading to or framing vistas or views created within the garden, or else 'borrowed' from the natural landscape beyond the confines of the garden. The visual effect is balanced and the harmonious placement of the various elements has a soothing effect, as the eye is never jarred by an unexpected curve or irregular shape. Quite often, the end of a main path, or the junction where paths cross, will be marked by a focal point such as a water feature.

One of the great attractions of a formal pool is the delight to be found in the reflections of the sky and surroundings in the water, so it is advisable to make the pool as large as you comfortably can. A formal pool can be created in even the tiniest urban garden, however, simply by removing a paving slab, excavating and installing a liner or other water-containing device. A little pool like this, its water exactly level with the surrounding paving and perhaps with a small jet playing in its centre, would also be a charming way of adding interest to a large expanse of terrace.

In formal gardens, water is used chiefly as a design element, rather than to provide a habitat in which to grow a collection of plants. To reflect the formality of their surroundings, formal pools are usually square, rectangular or circular. They can be either sunken, where the water and the immediate surrounding are on the same level, or else raised with a retaining wall. Sometimes, raised pools are topped with an ornamental well-head over which climbing plants can be trained.

Before the advent of pre-formed pool liners and butyl rubber sheeting, pools were most often made of poured concrete; many still are, and it is a good way to achieve the clean angles and perfect curves required by a formal design. However, erecting shuttering, mixing sufficient concrete and reinforcing it is not the easiest method, and the Raised Pool project (see pages 58–9) demonstrates how to build a rectangular raised pool using concrete walling blocks with a butyl liner sandwiched between them. Whichever method you choose, careful preparation is the key to success. It is essential to excavate angles accurately, to keep lines parallel and curves uniform, and to check levels constantly, since nothing looks worse than having one side of the pool surround higher than the other.

Keep the pool full as possible. This will avoid the distraction of a width of grubby liner showing around the top edge and also give the greatest expanse of reflective surface, and so contribute the maximum amount of visual interest.

The impact of a formal pool is greatly enhanced by the 'hard landscaping' that frames it. When choosing bricks, concrete or stone paving slabs, cobbles or tiles, look for a style and colouring that is sympathetic to the building materials used on the house. Paving stones are often especially suitable since they come in several sizes and finishes. They also have the practical advantage in that they can be set to overlap the pool edge, so hiding the liner. If these are beyond your budget, an effective edging can be made with pressure-treated timber. Although the treatment chemicals might leach from the wood into the pool, this is not a big problem if you don't intend to grow plants or have fish in the pool. If building a raised pool, consider making the retaining walls broad enough for occasional seating.

As long as you are prepared to clip the plants regularly, formal pools can be edged very successfully with evergreen or ever-grey plants: ivy (many variegated ivies would be useful), box, low-growing cotoneasters such as *Cotoneaster horizontalis* or *C. microphyllus*, dwarf lavenders (try 'Hidcote' or 'Munstead'), santolina, sage or thyme – anything that will respond to tight clipping or is naturally neat and hummocky. The project on pages 56–7, uses the evergreen *Pachysandra terminalis* to great effect.

Because the purpose of this type of water feature is purely structural, it should not be over-planted. A careful choice of plants, though, will reinforce the formality of the scheme. Seek out plants that have clearly defined shapes; if you read of a plant having 'architectural foliage' or 'sculptural form', chances are it will be the ideal complement for a formal water feature. But be restrained – one or two specimen plants is enough and try to choose them for the quality of their foliage rather than the brilliance of the flower colour. In general, limit the actual water plants to one or two choice waterlilies (*Nymphaea* 'James Brydon' is a luscious pink). Fish can seek shelter beneath the spreading foliage and the crisp-petalled flowers will enhance the ornamental nature of the pool.

The corners of a pool could be marked with pot-grown plants, an ideal summer setting for half-hardy plants. There are some wonderful reconstituted stone ornaments available, fashioned to look like baskets, or made in the shapes of classical urns. *Agave americana*, *Cordyline australis*, *Aeonium arboreum* or a clump of the umbrella palm, *Cyperus involucratus*, are just some of the spiky, tropical-looking plants that could be used to emphasize the sculptured element of the pool.

Sunken pools can be accented by the use of fastigiate or columnar trees like dwarf Irish juniper or even Italian cypress, which would succeed in the micro-climate of an enclosed town garden. Alternatively, select trees that have been trained as mop-headed standards. These could be small citrus trees as well as the familiar bay or box, which would look most attractive thanks to their glossy evergreen foliage – and the scent of the citrus flowers would be an added bonus.

The range of hardy foliage plants that could be used to complement a formal pool is extensive, but heading any list would be some of the big-leaved hostas such as 'Sum and Substance' or 'Big Daddy'. Ferns are frequently chosen for planting near a formal pool – *Dryopteris felix-mas* and *Polystichum setiferum* are particularly striking – but most do best with a degree of shade, so would not be suitable for a pool in the centre of a sunny stone-paved terrace. Other statuesque perennials that would associate well with a formal pool are *Ligularia* 'Desdemona', *Rheum palmatum* 'Atropurpureum', *Rodgersia podophylla* and, but this is not one for a small pool, *Gunnera manicata*. Use such bold-leaved plants sparingly, just one or two to create a visual counterpoint to the pool.

The corners of a raised pool provide attractive places for a variety of decorative elements, from simple acorn finials to well-stocked, colourful planters.

Sunken formal pool

Pool size: 2m (6ft) diameter

Materials

Rigid circular pre-formed unit
   2m (6ft) in diameter

½cu m (½yd) soft sand

12 aquatic planting baskets
   with fine or louvre mesh
   sides

2 x 25kg bags of aquatic
   compost

48 bunches of oxygenating
   plants

Small bag of pea shingle

24 evergreen groundcover
   shrubs

4 x 80-litre bags of tree and
   shrub planting compost

Sunken formal pools are best sited near the house, where their firm outline complements the architecture, and the soothing reflections and cooling effect of the still waters will be most easily enjoyed. The dark mysterious depths of a sunken pool, its water almost flush to the surrounding ground level, can be used to break the monotony of a paved terrace.

This simple pool uses a rigid pre-formed liner requiring no building skills. The water surface is clear of marginals and waterlilies but oxygenating plants are grown in the deep zone to keep the water clarified. A surrounding fringe of evergreen groundcover (Pachysandra terminalis has been used here) creeps over the edge to form a softening yet still formal frame.

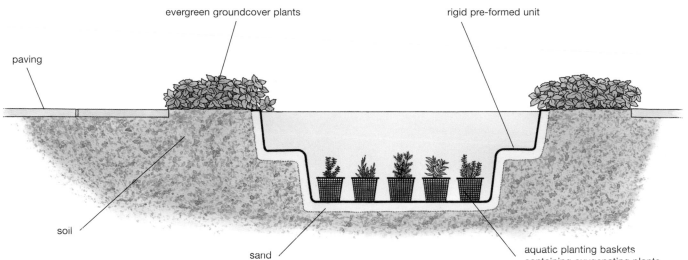

evergreen groundcover plants

rigid pre-formed unit

paving

soil

sand

aquatic planting baskets
containing oxygenating plants

Construction

1. Mark out the position of the pool by placing the rigid pool unit upside down on the site and marking out the outline with sand.

2. From 10cm (4in) outside the outline dig out the soil to the same depth as the marginal shelf of the unit.

3. Rake over the freshly dug soil.

4. Lift the unit into the hole and press down gently. The imprint made by the base of the deep zone will act as a guide to the next area to dig out.

5. From 10cm (4in) outside this imprint dig out the area to the full depth of the pool, allowing an extra 5cm (2in) for a bed of sand. You can check the depth of the hole by placing a straight edge across the sides of the hole and measuring from the straight edge to the bottom.

6. After raking over the base of the hole and removing any sharp stones from the base and sides, spread 5cm (2in) of sand over the bottom of the hole.

7. Lower the pool into place, pressing down gently. Check that the sides are level by placing a straight edge over the opposite sides and holding a spirit level on top. Do this over several places and if discrepancies in level are found, remove the pool and adjust the sand layer on the bottom.

8. Once satisfied that the pool sides are level all the way round, pour approximately 10cm (4in) of water into the bottom to give stability to the pool.

9. Begin backfilling the sides around the pool with sand, checking regularly that the unit remains level. Firm the sand around the sides by tamping with a thick stick or wooden handle. Continue to add more water as the backfilling proceeds, until the level reaches about 5–7cm (2–3in) from the top.

10. The aquatic baskets of oxygenators should be planted as soon as possible on the pool bottom. Use aquatic compost in the baskets and insert the bunches into each basket, planting them 2–3cm (1in) deep into the firmed compost. Topdress with pea shingle before immersing to prevent the soil from floating into the pool.

11. Fork the planting compost into the soil around the pool, extending out about 30cm (12in) – the plants will need a good start in life to cover as quickly as possible and achieve a close carpet of leaves.

12. Water the plants before planting. Plant into the enriched soil to the same depth as they were growing in their pots and then water thoroughly again after planting.

Raised pool

Size: approximately 2.4m (8ft) square and 45cm (18in) high

Materials

20 wooden pegs about 22cm (9in) long

150 concrete walling blocks 300 x 210 x 75mm (12 x 8 x 3in)

1cu m (cu yd) sharp sand

1cu m (cu yd) soft sand

1cu m (cu yd) 13mm (½in) ballast

4 x 25kg bags of cement

Flexible liner and underlay 3.6 x 3.6m (12 x 12ft)

30cm (12in) rigid polythene pipe 13mm (½in) diameter

28 coping stones 37cm (15in) square with bevelled edge

6–8 large decorative cobbles

Submersible pump with 30cm (12in) rigid delivery pipe 2.5cm (1in) in diameter

Galvanized metal grid 1.3m (4ft) square

A raised pool will make an emphatic visual statement in the garden, and can be used as a design marker, for example at the crossing point of main paths through a garden, as an eyecatching focal point or simply to provide a contemplative heart to a richly planted flower garden. In gardens where there are small children, a raised pool also has safety advantages (see pages 18–19).

The construction of this raised pool requires a high degree of building skills. Although the materials can alter in different styles of raised pool, the basic method of twin-wall construction with a liner sandwiched between remains the same.

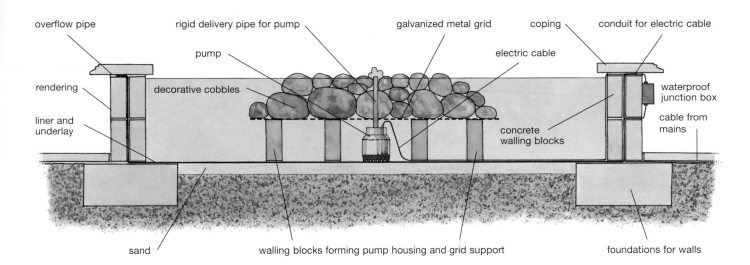

Labels on diagram:
overflow pipe · rigid delivery pipe for pump · galvanized metal grid · coping · conduit for electric cable · pump · electric cable · rendering · decorative cobbles · waterproof junction box · liner and underlay · cable from mains · concrete walling blocks · sand · walling blocks forming pump housing and grid support · foundations for walls

Construction

1. Mark out the outline of the pool with stakes and string.

2. Under the outline dig out a foundation trench 45cm (18in) wide and 20cm (8in) deep.

3. Insert the wooden pegs in the base of the trench so that their tops are about 2–3cm (1in) below ground level. Use a spirit level and straight-edged length of timber about 2m (6ft) long to check they are all level.

4. Mix a concrete foundation mix using 1 part cement to 6 parts ballast. Pour into the trench and tamp the wet concrete so that it is level with the top of the pegs. Leave to dry for at least 24 hours.

5. Lay the electric cable from the nearest supply to the foundations, leaving a metre or so of cable loose which will be incorporated later into the twin walls of the pool.

6. When the concrete foundations are dry, build the outer wall of two courses of concrete blocks. Mix up the mortar for the walls in small batches, using 1 part cement to 6 parts soft sand. The spare electric cable is fed through the wall from the inside between two blocks to be joined up to a waterproof junction box later (see diagram).

7. Spread an even layer of sand to a depth of 5cm (2in) over the bottom of the pool and drape the underlay and liner over it and up the sides. Smooth into position, pleating it neatly into the corners. Secure the liner temporarily on top of the wall with bricks.

8. Build the inner walls on top of the liner to the same height as the outer walls, sandwiching the liner between the walls to form a watertight seal.

9. Lay the coping stones on top of the two walls, embedding the liner at the same time into the mortar. Place a length of the rigid plastic pipe into the mortar immediately above the point where the electric cable has been threaded through below, to act as a conduit later for the pump cable. Incorporate a second length of pipe at another point under the coping to act as an overflow. Keep checking that the coping stones are laid level.

10. Inside the pool use one layer of walling blocks to build a square housing for the pump and to support a grid for the cobbles. Do not mortar these. Leave small gaps between the blocks to allow water movement to the pump and access for the electric cable.

11. Place the pump inside the housing. Drape the pump lead across the bottom of the pool, then through the conduit under the coping.

12. Connect the cables from the mains and the pump to a waterproof junction box.

13. Mix up rendering of 1 part cement and 4 parts sharp sand and apply to the outer walls to cover up the unattractive walling blocks.

14. Lay the metal grid on top of the framework and feed the rigid pipe from the pump through the grid. Arrange the cobbles on top of the grid to disguise the protruding pipe.

INFORMAL POOLS

'Back to nature' is the aim of many gardeners when they first set about cultivating their plots. For many, a natural garden would not be complete without a pool. Gardens, after all, can't exist without water, and the range of plants that positively demand a watery habitat is an exciting one to investigate. Then there is the wildlife that would be attracted to the garden by even the smallest pond.

The old adage is, 'Nature abhors a straight line' and informal pools most often mimic nature by having irregular outlines of gentle sweeping curves that are at ease in the densely planted settings of the wilder parts of the garden. In all but the smallest space it is possible to cultivate one corner to be a 'wild garden', and this is where the informal pool comes into its own. Unlike the formal pool, which contributes a strong, structural element to a garden's design, the informal pool is low-key and understated in comparison, and exists primarily to support water-loving plants and wildlife.

Small gardens tend to be square or rectangular flat plots bordered by hedges or panel fencing, so it can be daunting to try and ease a pool into the garden plan so that it looks as though it is part of the natural landscape. The transition from terrace or lawn to the water's edge must be made gradually, and this can be achieved by the way in which you develop the planting around the pool. Dense planting, obscuring part of the edge or one end of the pools, will help to give the impression that it is either fed by a stream or other natural source. One further step you can take to deceive the eye is to

The artificiality of this small pond is concealed by dense planting around its perimeter, using plants selected for their natural affinity to moist growing conditions.

build a shallow deck or bridge across one end of the pool; this will add a delightful air of mystery and illusion and also provide a vantage point from which to enjoy the tranquil scene.

From a practical standpoint, a natural-looking pool is easier to construct than a symmetrical formal pool. A flexible butyl liner or a pre-formed pool unit will give you the informal outline this sort of pool requires, or even a simple bowl or other attractive watertight container can serve.

Try to mimic nature in the way you use landscaping materials: choose all one type of stone if you want a rocky surround, and use smooth river gravel rather than crushed rock. Grade stones and pebbles to simulate a shingle slope into the water's depth or to form a landscaped apron well into the surrounding border. Large rocks carefully placed across the pool can act as stepping stones (but beware, they will soon become dangerously slippery) and plants spilling over the edge into the water will reinforce the natural look of the pool as well as disguise the liner.

Plants are an integral part of an informal water feature, but be guided in your choice of plants by considering the type of flower and foliage that occur naturally around ponds. Generally, the foliage will be quite bold and have strong shapes, and flowers will be softly coloured and small. And while a pretty feature can be made of one brightly coloured plant positioned to reflect in the water, collections of vibrantly coloured cultivars should be kept for other parts of the garden.

Although they will tolerate some shade, most water plants prefer open

Foliage form and texture are particularly strongly highlighted by the mirror reflections in the still water of this informal pool.

sunny positions. Fish, on the other hand, need shade. They also require deeper water than many plants do. As water warms, it will hold less oxygen, and on a sunny summer day, a couple of large fish in a small pond will use the available oxygen faster than it can be replenished by oxygenating water plants (see Submerged Plants, pages 114–17). Yet it is not a good idea to make a pond beneath trees; not only will the roots interfere with and possibly eventually damage the lining, but falling leaves in autumn will pollute the water.

Fulfilling the varying needs of water plants, fish and other pond life is a matter of providing a number of different habitats. This is quite possible even in a very small area, but does take a little thought and planning. Incorporate at least two different levels into the pond (see pages 64–5) and allow the sides to slope gently at first. A few half-submerged rocks by the water's edge will give a variety of pond-dwellers crevices to hide in and also provide an escape route for any small animals that might fall in by accident. At least part of the pool should be deep enough for fish to feel at home, and they can obtain shade from water plant foliage. A word of warning: if you intend to stock the pool with koi, the plants will need to be segregated since koi will uproot and eat the plants. If you construct the pool with a shelf fenced off from the main body of water, the plants can be grown at their proper depth in a protected habitat. Water plants aren't at risk from most other fish, and frogs and other amphibians and reptiles do little damage.

Maintenance of an informal pool is a matter of 'Less is more'. The great urge to tidy the pool in winter can be overwhelming, but remember that not only will fish, frogs and newts overwinter in the mud at the bottom of the pond, the cosy layer provides an abode for tiny creatures like waterfleas that are an important part of the food chain for pond-dwellers. And if you find the plants you have chosen are too rampant, take care when thinning them out, especially during summer when dragonfly nymphs, tadpoles and other youngsters are sheltering in the watery thickets.

Opposite: *Materials and plants must be carefully chosen for small informal ponds. The modest scale means that the detail of the finish is to the fore, as demonstrated by this stone-edged pool, planted with dainty waterlilies.*

Naturalistic pool for wildlife

Size: approximately 2.4 x 1.5m (8 x 5ft)

Materials

8 wooden pegs 15–22cm
    (6–9in) long

½cu m (½cu yd) soft sand

Flexible liner and underlay
    3.6 x 2.7m (12 x 9ft)

Approximately 20 rocks, each
    weighing about 20–25kg
    (50lb)

A little ready-mixed mortar
    (optional)

2 waterlilies

12 bunches of oxygenators

An informal pond, edged with mossy stones and overhung by simple flowering shrubs and ornamental foliage plants, will bring a soothing echo of nature into a quiet corner of the garden. Informal pools are the least complex to construct, but the skill comes in camouflaging the artifice. Look at the way natural ponds fit into their surroundings and observe how the forms of rocks, pebbles and gravel coalesce to create a sympathetic setting for a restrained palette of water-loving plants.

This system of construction, using a flexible liner, is one of the easiest and cheapest methods of making a small pool in an informal setting, and requires no building skills. The edge of the liner is disguised by rocks which should be even in size and shape and not too heavy to

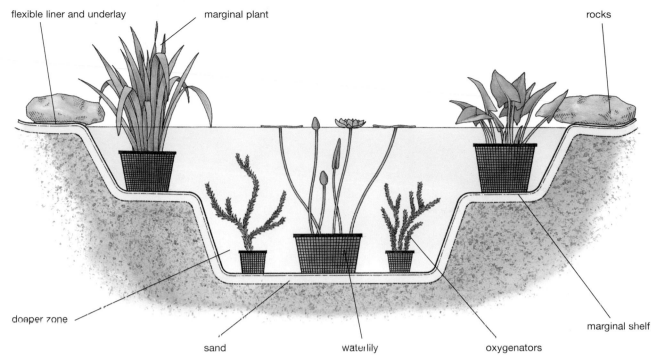

flexible liner and underlay   marginal plant   rocks

deeper zone

sand   waterlily   oxygenators

marginal shelf

allow easy adjustment. Make a slight overhang of rock over the water to help conceal the liner and provide shadow which makes the pool more interesting. A rock like sandstone, which retains moisture, will encourage moss to grow on it, which will further soften the appearance of the rocks. Planting in a slightly raised bed behind the rocks helps to link the rocky surround with the rest of the garden.

Construction

1. Mark out the position and shape of the pool with sand or string.
2. Knock in a peg at some point on the outline where the top of the peg will indicate the proposed finished water level.
3. Go round the outline and place pegs at 1–1.2m (3–4ft) intervals.
4. Knock in these pegs so that the top of each peg is level with the first peg. Use a spirit level to check the levels by resting it on a straight-edged piece of timber which is long enough to sit on the tops of adjacent pegs.
5. Dig out the entire area to a depth of 22–30cm (9–12in). Give the sides a gentle slope, so that they are not too steep for small animals to clamber up should they fall in.
6. Rake over the soil surface and mark out with sand an inner area at least 30cm (12in) inside the pool outline for the deeper zone.
7. Dig out the inner area to a finished minimum depth of 60cm (2ft). Rake over the floor and smooth the edges, removing any sharp stones.
8. Spread a layer of soft sand 2–3cm (1in) deep over the bottom.
9. Drape the underlay over the hole and firm into place. Drape the liner over it and press firmly into the contours, using stones or bricks to hold the edges temporarily in place.
10. Start pouring in water and as the water pressure gradually pushes the liner into place, pleat any large creases or folds before the weight of the water becomes too heavy.
11. When the water reaches 5–7cm (2–3in) below the proposed final level, place the edging stones informally on top of the liner, allowing the rocks to overlap the water slightly. Give the rocks extra stability and the liner a little more protection by placing the rocks on dabs of stiff mortar and pressing down firmly.
12. Plant oxygenators and waterlilies into aquatic baskets and place them on the bottom of the deeper zone, with baskets of marginal plants on the shallow shelf around the perimeter.

Tiny feature for an informal garden

Size of pool: 60 x 22cm (24 x 9in)

Materials

61 bricks

6–9 floor bricks

1 x 25kg bag of ready-mixed concrete

3 x 25 kg bags of ready-mixed mortar

1 x 25kg bag of rendering mortar mix

Small tin of waterproof sealant

4 bunches of oxygenating plants

Large decorative pot or planter

Informal pools don't have to be made of curves; sometimes it is the spirit of the pool that makes it informal. The right-angles and mortared brick edging of this tiny water incident may hint at formality, but its whimsical nature could not be more informal. Such miniature pools give an extra dimension to borders and mixed shrubbery.

The success of this feature depends upon it appearing an integral part of the planter and its base. There is not much bricklaying, but it is important that it is carefully done, with good mortar joints.

Waterproofing the small pool is achieved by rendering the inside of the brick walls with mortar and then painting with a waterproofing sealant. Without any planting there is a risk that the pool would

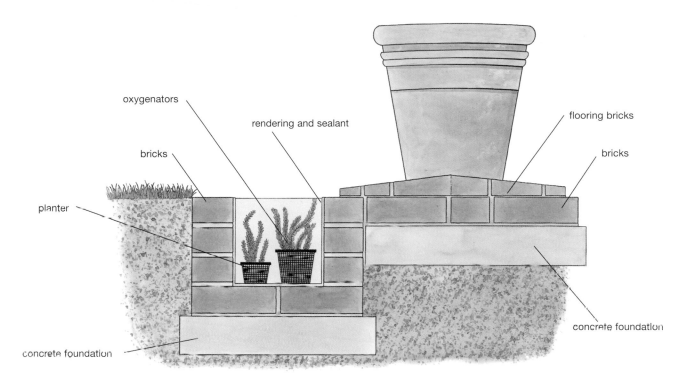

oxygenators

rendering and sealant

flooring bricks

bricks

bricks

planter

concrete foundation

concrete foundation

become cloudy; this can be remedied by planting with oxygenating plants or using chemicals such as algicides, otherwise frequent rinsing out with fresh water would be necessary.

Construction

1. Mark out the outline of the pool and plinth with strings and canes.

2. Dig out the rectangular area for the pool to a depth of 40cm (16in).

3. Add water to half the ready-mixed concrete to make a stiffish mixture. Spread a level layer 10cm (4in) thick over the base of the hole and allow to set for 24 hours.

4. Lay bricks flat side by side to form the base of the pool,

mortaring them on to the concrete foundation.

5. Build the side walls 3 bricks high, mortaring between the bricks, and allow 48 hours to set.

6. Dig out the adjacent area which will form a plinth for the pot to a depth of 17cm (7in). The size of the plinth should be kept in proportion to the rest of the feature. This one uses just 15 bricks to extend one long side of the pool, creating a base measuring 68cm (27in) square.

7. Add water to the remaining ready-mixed concrete for the plinth foundation and spread a level layer 10cm (4in) thick over the base of the hole.

8. Once it has set, mortar a layer of bricks on to the plinth foundation, arranging the bricks in a bonded pattern side by side. Mortar the joints between the bricks.

9. Complete the raised plinth by using the flooring bricks to form a diagonal square on top of the first layer.

10. Mix the ready-mixed rendering mortar with water to make a thick paste and render the inside walls of the small pool.

11. After allowing the rendering to dry for 48 hours, paint a waterproof sealant over the inside walls and allow to dry for a few hours.

12. Fill with water and place a pot of oxygenators on the bottom.

MOVING WATER
and still water

Moving water is a highly desirable feature for a small garden, since its presence adds a sensual dimension that will heighten the garden's soothing atmosphere – as long as the moving water is not a raging torrent! To have a natural stream running through your garden is a delight not many of us can boast, but there are a number of ways of bringing moving water into a garden. An artificial stream is really just a long thin pond with a pump installed to allow the water to flow from one end to the other before being pumped up an underground pipe to begin again. The challenge in something of this sort is making it appear a natural part of the surroundings, perhaps an unrealistic goal in the middle of a city or on a housing estate!

When planning an informal garden I find it useful to keep in mind that while I may turn to nature for inspiration, and I try to learn from nature how best to create a garden feature, I am not trying to *duplicate* nature – the effect I want is naturalistic; in other words, an interpretation of nature. In the case of moving water the vital thing is to disguise where the water is coming from. It would be entirely unsatisfactory simply to plonk a stretch of 'stream' down in the middle of the lawn. As with a naturalistic pool, the 'source' must be camouflaged, perhaps by screening one end of a stream behind a dense planting of water-loving perennials and small overhanging trees – the fine-leaved Japanese maples in their weeping or spreading forms are perfect for this. Alternatively, one end of the feature could be tucked under the paving of a terrace or planks of wooden decking while the other end could trickle off into the shrubbery.

More stylized, and so easier to assimilate into many settings, is a rill. A rill is to a stream what a canal is to a river: an obviously man-made, slow-moving ribbon of water in a straight narrow channel. It can flow between

The calming ripple and burble of moving water can be included in any suitable garden by using a simple rill, which is a single channel of water bordered by stone paving.

parallel strips of paving in a highly architectural fashion, or between banks of densely planted moisture-loving plants. Rills were a favourite device of Gertrude Jekyll and Edwin Lutyens; they often located the beginning of a rill near the house and directed it out into the garden, thereby forming a visual link between the building and its surrounding landscape. In a small town garden, a rill could be used in a similar fashion, beginning at a formal feature on the terrace or patio and then becoming gradually more informal as it reaches into the garden, eventually ending in a small, well-planted pool.

Falling water adds fascination to a garden and it is astonishing how much additional interest can be created by the addition of a small submersible pump. Water can then be directed across a platform that juts out over the pool, or can trickle between two small ponds on a sloping site. For more ambitious cascades, some pre-formed fibreglass units come close to emulating the shape of a natural waterfall but it is difficult to disguise the artificial nature of most materials; for preference try to use natural materials to construct a naturalistic falling water feature. In an urban or stylized

The still surface of the water combined with the strong shapes and textures of plants, pebbles and the pyramid sculpture create a stunning water feature.

setting, on the other hand, it is better to emphasize the artifice – the Urban Cascade on pages 72–3, for example, provides the attraction of falling water without any play at appearing as a natural occurrence.

Play with the sound of water. The rate of flow makes a great difference to the aural as well as the visual effect, so an adjustable valve is a useful tool (see page 36). The size of pebbles in the bottom of a stream or beneath falling water can also modulate its sound, as will obstacles

over which the water will flow, break and eddy. Experiment – it's the only way to realize the potential of moving water.

The reflective quality of water is also something to be exploited. Just as flowing water brings sound and movement to a garden, the perfect stillness of a mirror pool will exude light and tranquillity, and the dark mystery of a still sheet of water is wonderfully alluring.

Such a pool is strongly textural – imagine the almost tactile glassiness of the water surface harmonizing with an unbroken expanse of a large window or contrasting with a paved terrace or closely mown lawn.

Still water features can be used to great effect in confined spaces, in much the same way that some designers (both garden and interior) use mirrors to make the space seem larger. Many small town gardens have long narrow plots, and it is a an old trick to lay out the garden widthways to visually push the sides outwards. A still canal, laid across the width of the garden, near the house where the reflections can be immediately appreciated, will play the same visual trick, making the garden seem wider and larger.

The beauty of a reflecting pool or canal lies in the materials from which it is made, rather than the (few) plants which you may choose to grow around it. So it is worth spending just a bit more to have the pool well made from attractive and interesting materials – York stone slabs or blocks of slate instead of concrete slabs. The granite tiling around the pool in the project on pages 74–5 enhances its reflective qualities and emphasizes the purity of line of the design. In the gardens of the Hempel Hotel in central London three square still pools are set equidistant from each other into the central lawn. Each pool is bordered by a stone slab edging and simply outlined in white marble chippings. Planting is limited and stylized: the trees surrounding the pool are pollarded and the shrubs are topiary box balls. The minimalism is studied and meticulously executed – the only decorative ornament is the reflected clouds – but that is more about architecture than gardening.

Opposite: *A small splash of water highlights a shady corner. Modern pumps and kits allow you to create water features from even the simplest pots and crocks.*

An urban cascade

Size: 2m (6ft) wide and 2.4m (8ft) deep

Materials

24 wooden pegs about 22cm
    (9in) long
1cu m (cu yd) 2cm (¾in)
    ballast
6 x 25kg bags of cement
400–500 bricks
12 concrete walling blocks
    300 x 210 x 75mm
    (12 x 8 x 3in)
6 x 25kg bags of white
    decorative cobbles
Urn
Submersible pump
3.6m (12ft) flexible pipe
    13mm (½in) in diameter
Flexible liner and underlay
    2 x 2m (6 x 6ft)
54 quarry tiles 15cm (6in)
    square, including 9 with one
    round edge
Galvanized metal grid 60cm
    (2ft) square
2cu m (cu yd) rubble infill
4cu m (cu yd) sand
Decorative water spout

A rocky cascade or plunging waterfall would probably look out of place in most town gardens, but this combination of stylized waterfall and pebble pond provides all the attractions of flowing water tailored to suit an urban or modern setting. The overflowing terracotta pot adds a note of humour and increases the variety of water movement.

This innovative water feature requires a high degree of skill in bricklaying, but involves minimum maintenance once completed. The cobbles suspended over the lower pool not only hide the pump but exclude light from the reservoir of water below, helping to reduce algae.

Construction

1. Mark out the area with stakes and string and then dig out a trench for the foundations 45cm (18in) deep and 20cm (8in) wide. Prepare the trench with the depth-measuring pegs, mix the sand and ballast and pour the foundations as for Stages 3 and 4 of the Raised Pool (pages 58–9).
2. Construct the brick walls that form the outer perimeter of the feature, and the internal dividing wall. Incorporate in the back wall the flexible pipe that will deliver water from the pump in the lower pool up to the water spout, threading it between courses as shown in the diagram.
3. Before laying the top course

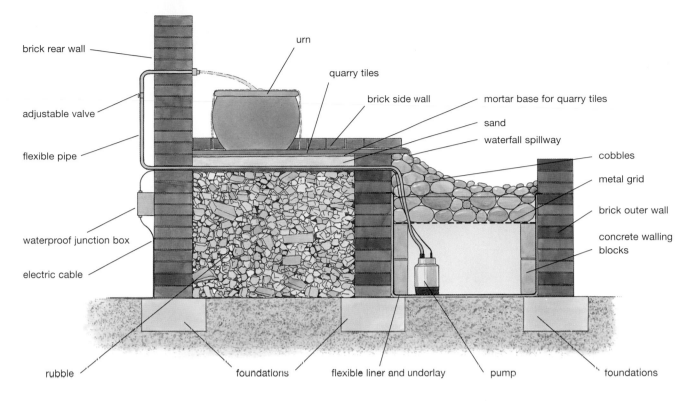

brick rear wall

adjustable valve

flexible pipe

waterproof junction box

electric cable

urn

quarry tiles

brick side wall

mortar base for quarry tiles

sand

waterfall spillway

cobbles

metal grid

brick outer wall

concrete walling blocks

rubble

foundations

flexible liner and underlay

pump

foundations

of brickwork around the pebble pool, spread 5cm (2in) of sand evenly over the bottom of the pool area and put in place the underlay and liner, smoothing and fitting as for the Raised Pool. Mortar the final course of bricks in place and leave all brickwork to dry for at least 24 hours.

4. Build the inner wall of the pebble pool with two courses of walling blocks, sandwiching the liner to form a waterproof seal.

5. Tip rubble infill into the rear half of the feature, until it is roughly 5cm (2in) below the top of the front wall. Spread over this a layer of sand 5cm (2in) deep. Lay the flexible pipe across the sand and gently press in until it is buried. Do the same with the electric cable from the pump. Firm

down the sand and smooth off level with the front wall.

6. Make up mortar with 1 part cement and 5 parts sand and mix to a reasonably stiff consistency. Spread the mortar over the sand and the top of front wall to a depth of 2–3 cm (1 in). Make sure that this bed of mortar is precisely flat and sloping very slightly towards the front. Lay on it the quarry tiles, finishing off with the round-edged tiles along the front.

7. Install the pump in the bottom of the pool – this complex feature places different demands on the pump and expert advice will be necessary to choose the right pump. Attach the lower end of the flexible pipe to the pump. An adjustable valve known as a gate valve should be fitted somewhere

along the pipe's length. This regulates water flow like a tap and, as frequent adjustment may be necessary, it should be fitted at a point where it is within easy reach.

8. Attach the water spout to conceal the upper end of the flexible pipe where it pokes through the back wall.

9. Connect the electric cables from the pump and the mains to a waterproof junction box.

10. Lay the metal grid over the lower pool to rest on the inner walling blocks. Fill with water to test the pump is working, then generously cover the grid with beach cobbles.

11. Place the urn in position and fill with water. Switch on the pump and adjust the water flow until the right effect is achieved.

Reflecting pool

Size: 2.1m (7ft) by 45cm (18in)

Materials

44 granite tiles 22cm (9in) square for pool interior, plus extra for surround

4 paving slabs 60cm (2ft) square

18 concrete walling blocks 300 x 210 x 75mm (12 x 8 x 3in)

2 x 25kg bags of ready-mixed rendering mortar

About 2 x 1m (6 x 3ft) plywood 2cm (¾in) thick

2 hinges

1 flush-fitting handle

Hardcore for foundations of surround

1 cu m (cu yd) ballast

4 x 25kg bags of cement

Small tube of mastic sealant

Waterproof sealant

Floor tile adhesive

40cm (16in) rigid plastic pipe 13mm (½in) in diameter

Submersible pump

Ultra-violet clarifier

2m (6ft) flexible pipe 13mm (½in) in diameter

4 hose clips 13mm (½in) in diameter

Water can be used to bring life and space to difficult areas like the side access or narrow passage to a back door. In truly small 'postage-stamp' gardens a sheet of water has the same effect as a mirror, capturing the light, expanding the perimeter and adding depth.

It is vital with formal reflecting pools that the water is kept in pristine condition without any planting to clutter the water surface. Some system of filtration is therefore essential and here a small pump circulates water through an ultra-violet clarifier. The circulation rate is kept low to prevent water turbulence. The water level should be level with the surrounding tiles.

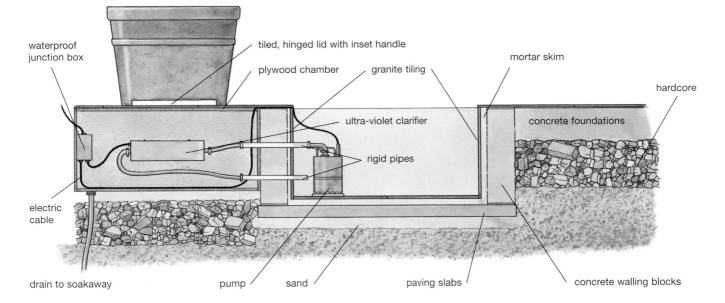

waterproof junction box

tiled, hinged lid with inset handle

plywood chamber

granite tiling

mortar skim

hardcore

ultra-violet clarifier

concrete foundations

rigid pipes

electric cable

drain to soakaway

pump

sand

paving slabs

concrete walling blocks

Construction

1. Mark out the pool area with strings and canes, allowing an extra 22cm (9in) to the length and to the width to provide space for four paving slabs which will act as the base of the pool and as foundations for the side walls. Dig out this area to a depth of 30cm (12in).

2. Spread a layer of sand 2–3cm (1in) thick over the bottom of the pool hole. Ensure it is level and lay on it the paving slabs side by side.

3. Use the concrete walling blocks to build the side walls of the pool on the paving slabs.

4. Coat the base and side walls with an even coat of rendering and leave a day or two to dry.

5. Dig out the area outside the pool walls to a depth of 22cm (9in). Spread a layer of hardcore 7cm (3in) deep over the base.

6. Make a plywood box with a hinged lid as a chamber for the ultra-violet clarifier. If necessary, use angle brackets for strengthening.

Include a small drain in the bottom so that water cannot collect and short the clarifier. Paint with waterproof sealant.

7. Position the box against a longer side of the pool, nestling it down into the hardcore so that the lid is level with the top of the wall.

8. Cover with a concrete foundation mix (1 part cement to 6 parts ballast) to bring up level with the pool walls. Smooth carefully and leave for a week.

9. Paint the rendered interior of the pool with a waterproof sealant and allow to dry.

10. Stick the granite tiles to the pool's base and sides and the prepared surround with a strong tile adhesive, using a heavy-duty tile cutter when necessary. When tiling the lid of the clarifier's chamber be careful not to impede the hinges. Incorporate the lifting handle at a convenient point, ensuring it is flush with or below the surrounding tiles.

11. Drill two holes just large enough for the 13mm (½in) pipe to pass through the pool walls into the plywood chamber. They should be about 10cm (4in) below the water surface and as far apart as possible to create a gentle but inconspicuous current. Feed lengths of the rigid pipe through the holes, leaving 5–7cm (2–3in) protruding from each side, and seal around them with mastic sealant and a coat of waterproof sealant.

12. Install the clarifier in the chamber and attach its flow and return pipes to the rigid piping with hoseclips.

13. Grout all tiling with a waterproof grout, then give the grouted tiles a further coat of sealant.

14. Install the pump, ideally raising it slightly off the floor of the pool with an offcut of tile. Connect it to the clarifier and electricity supply via a waterproof junction box.

15. Fill the pool to the brim and switch on the pump and clarifier.

Moving Water and Still Water   75

STONE
and pebble features

A collection of curiously shaped rocks forms the foundation for this intriguing bubble fountain. The constant film of water playing over their surfaces highlights the individual beauty of each stone.

It can be difficult to fit an informal water feature into a small city garden; the immediate environs are so emphatically man-made that any attempt at creating a naturalistic pool will be fraught with difficulty. To be effective, such pools require adequate space for water and marginal plantings, and room to disguise the artificial nature of the pool's construction. When your neighbour's washing can be seen over the panel fencing or brick wall and the sky above is festooned with telephone wires, it is hard to pretend you are in some sylvan glade. In such a setting, or in any small space, a shallow, pebble-lined pool filled with just enough water to keep the stones wet, or a bubble fountain set into a stone-covered section of terrace will be much more convincing, thanks to its simplicity.

There are many reasons to choose a stone or pebble water feature: they tend to be smaller in scale than other features and so are ideally suited to gardens where space is at a premium; they are not imposing, so they can easily be incorporated into any planting scheme; the shapes, sizes and colours of the stone can be varied to suit any criteria, and the finished feature will have a sculptural quality lacking in most other features. A shallow pool filled with large pebbles poses less of a hazard than an open pool so is a better, safer choice if young children play in the garden. But above all these worthy considerations, who can resist the prettiness of water-washed pebbles?

Pebble and stone water features are usually constructed at ground level and positioned as a focal point; a butyl liner, a pre-formed pool unit, an old shower tray or any shallow receptacle that will hold water can be filled with pebbles. An alternative is to make the container part of a raised bed or to erect the container on a brick plinth or pedestal – ready-made fountains, half-barrel tubs, pre-formed concrete 'saucer' pools can all be converted to pebble features.

A pebble pool could also add interest to an adjacent 'full' pool, be sited below a water spout or include a fountain. If a fountain is to be part of the design, the container below will need to be deep enough to house a small pump, but it is not necessary to stack the container to the brim with pebbles – a sturdy wire-mesh grid can be placed across it and then covered with pebbles, with the plumbing hidden below.

Installing a pump opens up the range of possibilities. Fountain nozzles come in a wide range, shaped to give different effects, such as bells. Choose one of the bubble variety; a spray or jet fountain will look like a geyser erupting! I have seen a cheery little feature made from an 'ever-dripping tap' that leaks on to a puddle of pebbles – the tap is, of course, linked to a pump.

A variation of this theme, but using one giant stone instead of a collection of smaller cobbles, is the millstone. Garden centres offer a range of simulated 'millstones'; some of these can look fairly realistic, but just as many look like what they are – cold slabs of dull grey cast concrete. Choose with care and discretion. It will also help to see one linked to a water feature, as whatever material is used, it will look very different under the sheen of water.

Remember when selecting the stones that the finished feature will be like a piece of sculpture, so go for attractively coloured cobbles, or ones that are especially nicely shaped and do try to limit the variety of types of stone you include. Think of a pebble beach or a stone-banked stream; the materials there would be homogenous.

As far as planting is concerned, this type of feature presents the perfect opportunity to grow moisture-loving plants (unless you are including a fountain, in which case plants should be kept to the surrounding area). The pebbles can be laid on a moisture-holding compost mix, providing a habitat ideally suited to plants like *Houttuynia cordata*, astilbes, primulas and other moisture-lovers (see pages 122–6). In a mild, sheltered garden, *Lobelia cardinalis* and *Zantedeschia aethiopica* would also enjoy this site.

Water gushes from a pipe into a shallow pebble pool. As in nature, the pebbles for this feature have a uniformity of shape, colour and texture

Millstone bubble fountain

Size: 90cm (3ft)

Materials

Fibreglass millstone kit
including moulded reservoir
surround 90cm (36in)
square with deeper central
sump area

Submersible pump with rigid
PVC or polythene outlet
pipe approximately
30–45cm (12–18in) long

Selection of washed rounded
cobbles

Even the smallest city garden can enjoy the benefit of a water feature when it has the sculptural qualities of a millstone fountain. Surrounded by moisture-loving plants, the ridged, worn appearance of the millstone's surface and the informal jumble of cobbles on which it sits create a pleasing series of contrasts. The sight and sound of the small bubble fountain adds another dimension to the composition, which would be ideally suited to a sheltered corner.

Real millstones are now hard to come by in most places, are often expensive and extremely heavy. Fibreglass versions, such as the one used here, are an attractive alternative now that the reproduction has improved so much, and they soon weather to look even more natural. They are also light and easy to manoeuvre, which makes installation very much easier.

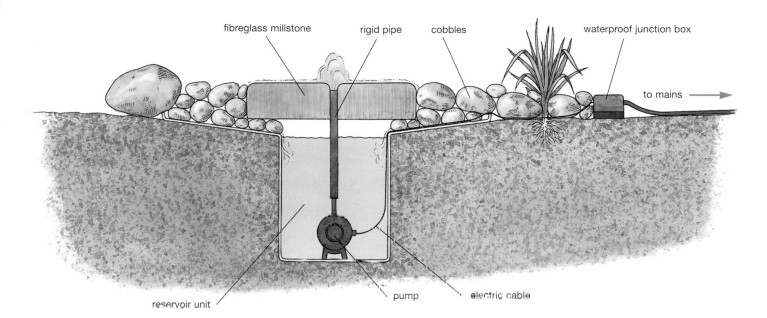

fibreglass millstone   rigid pipe   cobbles   waterproof junction box

to mains →

reservoir unit   pump   electric cable

Construction

1. Mark out a level site in a suitable focal point in a border or an area of paving.

2. Measure the depth of the reservoir sump and surround and dig out a hole to the same dimensions as the unit.

3. Position the reservoir unit in the hole. Check that it is level by placing a spirit level on top of a straight-edged piece of timber which rests on opposite sides of the reservoir rim. If any correction has to be made, lift out the unit and adjust the excavation accordingly.

4. Place the pump in the sump and connect the pump lead and the mains supply to a waterproof junction box which can be disguised by planting or rocks.

5. Place the length of rigid pipe on to the pump outlet. (This is normally supplied with most pump kits.)

6. The millstone has a central hole which allows it to be dropped over the rigid pipe. When the millstone is in place, check the pipe does not stick out above the millstone. If it is too long, remove the millstone and take off the excess with a hacksaw.

7. Replace the millstone, fill the sump with water and turn on the pump. The rate of water flow emerging from the centre of the millstone can be adjusted to the desired level by turning off the pump, lifting off the millstone and adjusting the flow rate adjustor on the outlet of the pump. Replace the millstone and restart the pump.

8. The rippling effect of the water over the millstone surface requires the millstone to be exactly level. Make any necessary adjustment to the millstone by wedging small pebbles between the reservoir surround and the underside of the millstone rim.

9. Arrange the washed rounded cobbles around the sides of the millstone, extending them beyond the reservoir surround so that plants can grow between the cobbles for a more informal effect.

Pebble pond

Size: 2 x 2m (6 x 6ft)

Materials

Flexible liner and underlay
   2.4 x 2.4m (8 x 8ft)
Logs, bridge or timber decking
Submersible pump
2m (6ft) of flexible pipe 13mm
   (½in) in diameter
Ultra-violet clarifier
10 x 25kg bags washed round
   beach cobbles

Shallow pebble ponds are easy to make. They fit neatly into tiny town gardens or can be used to make an impression in larger gardens where you might ordinarily expect to find a more substantial pool. Little features such as this are best sited near to the house and can be incorporated into the patio paving. The play of reflections on the water surface, fragmented by the textured contours of the pebble-lined pool, contribute to the pronounced sculptural quality of a pebble pond, a quality it shares with the Millstone Bubble Fountain (see pages 78–79).

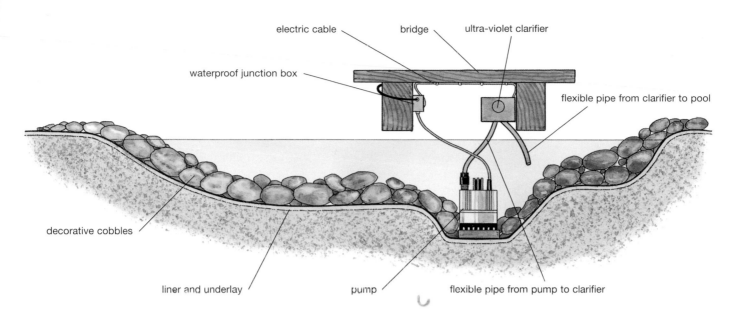

electric cable — bridge — ultra-violet clarifier

waterproof junction box

flexible pipe from clarifier to pool

decorative cobbles

liner and underlay — pump — flexible pipe from pump to clarifier

While the basic construction of a pebble pool is relatively easy, some means of keeping the water clear must be considered, as the large expanse of shallow water with no planting makes such pools prone to greening. Apart from regular changing of the water, which is wasteful and time-demanding, there are two main methods of keeping shallow pebble pools clear. The first method, involving the circulation of water through an ultra-violet clarifier, is described in the construction sequence below. The clarifier and the pump need to be hidden from view and in this rural setting, this has been achieved with the help of a simple plank bridge. A ready-built wooden bridge, timber decking or an ornamental duck house are just some of the alternative ideas to disguise the 'mechanics'.

A second method is to link the pebble pond with a much larger volume of water so that the pebble pool has the benefit of the deeper clearer water. A small hump in the pool contours below water level at the junction of the two pools is sufficient to prevent the cobbles from rolling into the deeper water.

Construction

1. Mark out the outline of the pool with canes and string.

2. Dig out a shallow saucer shape, making a small area deep enough to act as a sump for a small pump which will be hidden by the overhang of the bridge.

3. Rake over the excavation, removing any sharp stones.

4. Drape the underlay and then the liner into the hole, pushing the liner firmly into the sump. Hold the edges in place with a few large cobbles.

5. Install the bridge (or whatever alternative you have chosen), ensuring it is firmly fixed in position.

6. Place the pump into the sump and fix the ultra-violet clarifier to the underside of the bridge. Connect the pump outlet to a flexible pipe which in turn is connected to the clarifier.

7. Connect the flexible pipe to the outlet of the clarifier back to the pool. Connect the pump cable and the clarifier cable to a waterproof junction box near the pool.

8. Spread the cobbles over the entire surface of the liner, ensuring all piping is well hidden and heaping the cobbles up in places to well above the proposed water line.

9. Fill with water to the required depth, checking that the clarifier is above the water line. Trim off any excess liner once you are sure there is adequate depth of water. Turn on the pump and clarifier.

WALL FOUNTAINS
and water spouts

Of all the water features that are suited to small gardens, few are as classically elegant as the traditional mask and basin fountain. From their earliest appearances in the ornate gardens of ancient Rome to their use in gardens at the leading edge of contemporary design, this style of water feature is as valued for its adaptability as for its highly decorative nature.

In a small garden, the perimeter walls or fences are all too obvious. You

can disguise them with climbers, shroud them in trelliswork, or hang mirrors on them. But although concealment is one choice, using a wall to support a water feature would make a virtue of the vertical plane, and incorporate it honestly and openly into the garden design.

Any vertical surface might provide a suitable site for a wall mask or water spout. A house wall, with access to both sides, would make installation simpler than on a perimeter wall, or a wall can be specially constructed for the purpose – a cavity wall or a false wall in front of an existing wall would allow you to conceal the workings (electric cables, pipework and so on) at the time of construction. Fences and trellising are other possiblities as long as the feature, once in place, does not look at odds with its surroundings.

Water spouts, whether left plain or incorporated into a decorative mask or plaque, suit both formality and informality. In a formal garden plan they make ideal focal points, perhaps at the end of a path or other prominent spot, while they make a charming surprise amidst a riot of informal planting. In either setting the surrounding planting can be quite luxurious, using plants that will revel in the damp micro-climate created by the falling water: ferns, small-leaved ivies, hostas, astilbes, sweet woodruff, primulas and trollius would all make suitable neighbours.

The most basic type of mask is the all-in-one, moulded variety, in which mask and basin are formed as one unit. Installation requires no more than fixing the unit with screws or brackets to a firm vertical support and connecting the electric pump to an adjacent waterproof switch; the cabling, pump and so on can be concealed by plants or some other appropriate disguise. A self-contained unit like this can be installed in even the most confined spaces, such as basement courtyards, balconies, conservatories or even indoors to provide an unusual addition to the interior decor. Indoors or in a conservatory a nearby standard electric socket will be adequate.

Alternatively, you can purchase the mask and basin as separate items, which allows you to install the mask at any height above the basin. More ambitious still is a mask fountain that plays into a raised pool; again, you can adjust the height. The Wall Fountain on pages 86–7 shows how a mask and basin can work in combination with a pool.

Attention to detail is especially important in a small space, and in choosing a mask and basin there are several factors to bear in mind. The first is aesthetic. When considering a purchase, ask yourself: What will it look like in my garden? Can I live with looking at this every day? You may be surprised by the answer. Masks are

In contrast to the fountain opposite, this classical mask and basin fountain, complemented by Rosa *'New Dawn' and* Clematis *'Doctor Ruppel', is the main garden feature.*

available in a wide variety of images and materials: cherubs, Neptune faces with curling beards and flowing tresses, mermaid faces with equally luxuriant locks (but without a beard, or course!), lions, rams, fishes and so on. When considering a figurative mask in particular, check that it will conceal the nozzle successfully – you wouldn't want a cherub to look as if he was smoking a cigar!

Standards of artificiality are improving all the time, and features like this can be made in fibreglass, plastics, cast concrete and reconstituted cast stone as well as carved stone and ceramic, but quality varies enormously: some materials coloured to emulate lead, for example, are sometimes dyed a rather unconvincing grey.

Use the quietest pump you can obtain – you don't want to lose the sound of the playing water beneath a mechanical drone. The water itself should play in a musical trickle, so avoid powerful pumps that force the water out in a torrent – it will sound like someone has left the bath running. If there is no facility for adjusting the flow rate on an integral pump then it is worth experimenting with the depth of water in the basin or the addition of other materials to the reservoir. Shells are not only decorative but, being hollow, give an echoing effect, like water falling in a cave. Nozzles that emit the water in a gently spreading fan also sound different and can be quite attractive as the light refracts through the spray.

In a small basin you may need to use one of the proprietary chemicals on the market which have been formulated to prevent build-up of algae and bacteria in features with small water volumes.

A final and dramatic touch would be the use of spotlights, either highlighting the mask, or diffused against the background, but aim for a subtle effect that will enhance the display rather than overwhelm it (see pages 17–18 for more ideas on lighting).

A water spout does not, of course, have to be in the shape of a decorative mask. It can be used in a number of imaginative ways, from feeding a traditional water pump to a novelty feature like an ever-gushing watering can. In the Japanese Spill Basin on pages 88–9 the spout itself has become the focus, constructed from a length of stout bamboo to create a feature in the style of a Japanese *tsukubai*.

Basins and water form part of the traditional Japanese tea ceremony and the purification rites of the Shinto religion. Basins are low on the ground so that it is necessary to kneel (a sign of humility) to cleanse your hands, and the word *tsukubai* means to bend or kneel. The materials from which the water spout is made are the simplest possible: a length of bamboo and a rock on which there is a natural depression to serve as the basin. Large flat rocks placed around the small pool are knelt upon to reach the falling water and to rest drinking vessels and so on.

Japanese style features need careful placing in a sheltered and shady part of the garden, where planting is kept to simple groups of foliage plants like ferns and hostas, and ideally surrounded by a collection of mossy rocks.

There are several other Japanese-style water features suited to small gardens. One, the *shishi odoshi* or *sozu*, was originally intended as a deer-scarer. It is made from counterbalanced lengths of hollow bamboo. A stream of water is fed from a tank into a bamboo conduit balanced on a fulcrum above a stone. As the water collects in one end of the bamboo cane, it tips down to empty, making a resonating 'thunk' that can be heard throughout the garden. There are other Japanese bamboo water music-makers but the deer-scarer is the one now widely available in kit form from garden centres.

Water features for Japanese-style garden settings should have an uncomplicated design and be made of natural materials. This approach should be observed throughout because, in Japanese gardens, less really is more.

Wall fountain

Size: variable

Materials

Decorative spout or mask

Wall basin

Flexible pipe 13mm (½in) in
  diameter (length will
  depend on design)

60–75cm (2–2½ ft) copper
  pipe 13mm (½in) in
  diameter

4 hoseclips to fit piping

Submersible pump

This lion's head and shell basin illustrate beautifully how classical subjects do not necessarily need a formal, classical planting to complement them. The sandstone blends well with the arid Mediterranean plants and cacti, while the gentle splash of water accentuates the feel of a miniature desert oasis.

A wall fountain with a separate reservoir basin requires a little more work than an all-in-one unit, but installation is still straightforward if you have a ready-made wall with access to the back. A mask and basin combination works well with other water features; here, for example, the basin has been allowed to overflow into a small pool below, creating a modest double cascade.

Construction

1. Mark on the wall the outline of the mask or spout and the basin or reservoir.

2. Use a large masonry bit to drill two holes through the wall where the water pipe will emerge. Cut two lengths of copper pipe and insert them through the holes, leaving 5–8cm (2–3in) protruding either side. Use the hoseclips to attach the flexible piping to the copper pipes from the rear (see diagram).

In situations where it is difficult to work behind the wall, you could build a small false wall immediately in front of the existing wall, securing the basin into the new wall as it is built. An alternative is to fix trelliswork to the wall with battening. This provides an easy means to hide pipework and at the same time provides a framework for climbing plants to grow up.

3. Fix the basin securely to the wall; when full of water, a stone basin will be extremely heavy. If you are unsure your wall or fencing will take the strain, you might consider alternatives such as a stone bowl raised on a pedestal, or an attractive old sink or tank on the ground.

4. Fix the mask in place over the upper piece of copper pipe, concealing the end of the pipe as neatly as possible.

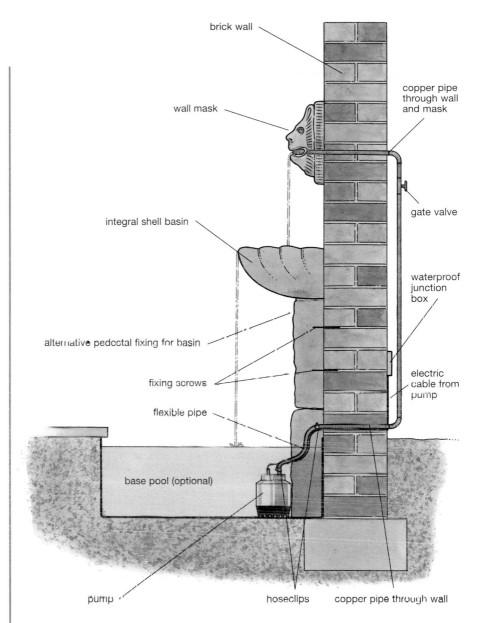

brick wall

wall mask

copper pipe through wall and mask

gate valve

integral shell basin

waterproof junction box

alternative pedestal fixing for basin

fixing screws

electric cable from pump

flexible pipe

base pool (optional)

pump

hoseclips

copper pipe through wall

5. Install the pump either in the basin or in a second reservoir below. Use the flexible pipe and a hoseclip to connect the pump to the lower copper pipe and connect the pump's electric cable to a waterproof junction box.

6. The water flow may take a lot of adjusting to get just the right effect – it is very easy for wall fountains, especially shallow ones, to sound like a dripping tap. If it can be attached at an easily accessible point, an adjustable (gate) valve on the pipework makes regulating the water flow easier.

Japanese spill basin

Pool: 1m (3ft) in diameter

Materials

Flexible liner and underlay
  2 x 2m (6 x 6ft)
12–15 rounded edging stones
  of sandstone or other soft
  stone which will gather
  moss easily
Basin stone about 30–40cm
  (12–16in) high with
  hollowed out saucer
  depression in the top
45–60cm (18–24in) length of
  hollow bamboo cane 2.5cm
  (1in) in diameter
2 strong bamboo canes
  approximately 1m (3ft) long
1 x 25kg bag of ready-mixed
  concrete
2m (6ft) flexible pipe 2.5cm
  (1in) in diameter
2 x 2.5cm (1in) hoseclips
Submersible pump
Ferns

The tsukubai fountain and basin forms part of the traditional Japanese tea ceremony, when it is used for ritual ablutions. In western gardens it would lose its cultural connotations, but by siting it near the house the fountain could still be used to rinse your hands after gardening or to provide a cool drink of clean water on a warm summer's day. Try to keep the surrounding planting simple. Choosing a shady, sheltered spot will encourage moss to grow on the large rocks which form part of the fountain ensemble.

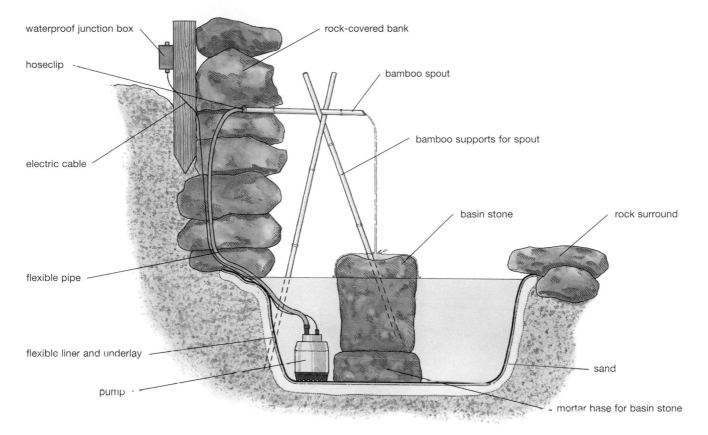

waterproof junction box

hoseclip

electric cable

flexible pipe

flexible liner and underlay

pump

rock-covered bank

bamboo spout

bamboo supports for spout

basin stone

rock surround

sand

mortar base for basin stone

Construction

1. Dig out a hole approximately 45cm (18in) deep (depending on the depth of the basin stone) and 1m (3ft) across. Check that the sides of the hole are level by placing a straight-edged piece of timber across the hole with a spirit level on top.

2. Insert the underlay then the flexible liner into the hole, firming into place by hand.

3. Check the height of the basin stone to see what height of foundation support is required to lift approximately 15cm (6in) of stone above the water.

4. Add just enough water to the ready-mixed concrete to make it workable but firm enough not to collapse under the weight of the basin stone. Make a mound on top of the liner where the stone will sit.

5. While the concrete is still moist, place the basin stone on top and firm gently, checking that the sides of the basin are roughly level.

6. Place rocks around the sides of the pool on the edge of the liner so that they slightly overlap the water. Build the rocks up the bank on one side of the pool. If necessary, secure the base with mortar.

7. Wedge the length of hollow bamboo cane between the rocks above the pool so that it slopes gently towards the pool. Leave the final fixing of it until it has been connected to the pump.

8. Install the pump in the pool and attach the flexible pipe to it with a

hoseclip. Run the flexible pipe up between and behind the rocks and connect it to the end of the bamboo spout with a hoseclip.

9. Pour enough water into the pool to allow the pump and the angle of the bamboo spout to be tested. Connect the pump cable to a waterproof junction box hidden behind the rocks.

10. Adjust the flow regulator of the pump or move the position of the bamboo spout so that water flow is directed into the saucer of the basin stone. Secure the pipe into the rocks by wedging stones around it and support the free end of the spout with two bamboo canes.

11. Top up the pool and plant ferns into gaps between the rocks.

SPLASH
fountains

S plash fountains, where the water sprays up from a nozzle and falls back into a pool, allow the water garden-maker a chance to introduce a humorous touch or a note of classical calm, depending upon the overall feel of the garden and the mood you wish to create. One of the most spectacular splash fountains I have ever encountered is in the sunken gardens at the Villa Torrigiani, near Lucca. Built in the seventeenth century, it combines frivolity with classical architecture in the huge water joke of the Temple of Flora. Inside the domed temple, water suddenly begins to gush and spray from the statues lining the walls, reaching a crescendo with the statue of Flora crowning the temple dome – water begins to pour from the garlands and basket of flowers she carries on her head, drenching anyone foolish enough to linger in the cool confines of the temple.

Contemporary gardens, and pockets, are unlikely to accommodate such grandiose effects, but the same lively spirit can be harnessed by siting prettily made statues plumbed for fountain use in unexpected corners of the garden, or else positioning them where the spray of water can be best appreciated – next to a patio or at a natural focal point.

There are so many splash fountain styles to choose from that it helps to consider the effect you want to achieve.

In its simplest form a fountain is a single jet of water spraying out of a pool or basin. This can be embellished in countless ways, from a few large waterworn rocks arranged to conceal the nozzle to a life-size Baroque statue or an abstract creation made out of recycled metal.

If you are choosing a statue the first rule is, don't stint. Select a well-made one that won't flake in frost and has features that are clearly modelled and well-defined – many cast-concrete efforts

Quality is vital when selecting a statue to form the focus of a splash fountain. Be sure that the figure is well modelled and carefully made, and that the materials and manufacture are natural-looking and sturdy.

look like so much misshapen clay. Secondly, figurative fountains will look well if they look believable.

Conventional stone statues are only one possibility, for there are fountain ornaments to suit any style or budget, so explore the great variety now available. Look for ideas in magazines and design books, in other people's gardens and at gardening shows. The part-cascade, part-fountain on pages 94–5 illustrates how a material not usually associated with fountains can be put to imaginative use.

A fountain does not have to be limited to a single spray. Slightly higher up the evolutionary ladder is the multi-jet spray which looks rather like an inverted shower, or a series of jets arranged in a row can form an attractive water screen. A magnificent example of this style was designed by the late Sir Geoffrey Jellicoe, one of England's foremost landscape architects, for the water parterre at Ditchley Park in Oxfordshire. To the side of the mansion a large formal water canal ends in a gentle curve lined with water jets that when in play formed a glittering curtain of water, screening the distant view of the deer park.

There is no reason why this flamboyant effect could not be scaled down for use in a small garden: a row of five or six jets 30cm (12in) long could be arranged across a narrow pool at the end of a path or some other place where a screen of water would be desirable. Incidentally, the Renaissance Italian garden made much use of such jets, and in Flora's garden at the Villa Torrigiani, water jets are placed along the stair risers descending into the garden and also across the paths, so that water literally chases you through the garden.

It's always worth investigating how things were done in the past, particularly in gardening, as a source of inspiration for what can be done in the present. The thing is not to *copy* the form, but to let the spirit of the past *inspire* your efforts.

Splash fountains can shape jets of water into some very unusual displays, like this shimmering, jellyfish-like spray playing over a carpet of pennywort.

Spray fountain

Size of pool: 2.4m (8ft) in diameter

Materials

Circular fibreglass pre-formed
    unit 2.4m (8ft) in diameter
½cu m (½cu yd) sand
Submersible pump with spray
    nozzle connection and rigid
    pipe outlet
8 concrete walling blocks
Galvanized metal grid on
    which fountain ornament
    can stand
Fountain ornament

Fun and games come into the water garden with the use of splash fountains; the play of water, the glitter and sparkle of the jets as they rise and fall have an exciting and entertaining quality which is heightened by the use of sculptured accompaniments like this circle of frogs, rejoicing in the fountain spray. Splash fountains can be positioned in the middle of a pool or along its side, but remember that on windy days the spray will reach quite a long way – which may be part of the effect.

This strong pre-formed fibreglass fountain pool is both easy to install and strong enough to support the weight of the fountain ornament without foundations under the pool. The main installation detail lies in achieving a strong base within the pool at the exact height to support the frogs and sculptured lily pads.

Construction

1. Mark out the outline of the pre-formed pool by turning it upside down and inscribing its outline in sand.

2. From 10cm (4in) outside the outline, dig out the soil to 5–7cm (2–3in) deeper than the marginal shelf of the unit.

3. Rake over the freshly dug soil. Lift the pool into the hole and press down gently. The base of the deeper zone of the pool will make an imprint on the raked soil which will act as a guide to the next area to be dug out.

4. From 10cm (4in) outside this imprint dig out the area to the full depth of the pool, removing an extra 5cm (2in) of soil to allow for a bed of soft sand. You can check the depth of the hole by placing a straight-edged piece of timber across the sides of the hole and measuring from the straight edge to the bottom.

5. After raking over the bottom of the hole and removing any sharp stones from the base and sides, spread a 5cm (2in) layer of soft sand evenly over the bottom, raking the sand as level as possible.

6. Lower the pool into place and press down gently. Check that the sides are level by placing a straight-edged piece of timber over the

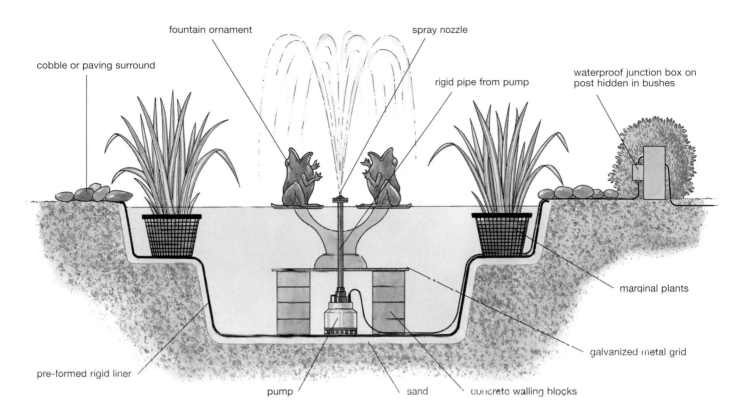

cobble or paving surround

fountain ornament

spray nozzle

rigid pipe from pump

waterproof junction box on post hidden in bushes

marginal plants

galvanized metal grid

pre-formed rigid liner

pump

sand

concrete walling blocks

opposite sides and holding a spirit level on top of the timber. Do this over several places and if discrepancies in level are found, remove the pool and adjust the sand layer on the bottom.

7. Once satisfied that the pool sides are level all the way round, pour approximately 10cm (4in) of water into the pool to give it stability.

8. Begin backfilling the sides around the pool with sand, checking regularly that the unit remains level. Firm the sand around the sides by tamping with a thick stick or wooden handle. Add another 7–10cm (3–4in) of water

as you go, to further increase the stability of the pool.

9. The ornamental fountain unit may need elevating from the pool bottom to allow the ornamental lily pads and frogs to sit on the surface. Concrete walling blocks laid flat on the pool base will give the necessary rigidity and height and at the same time provide a housing for the submersible pump.

Lay the galvanized metal grid across the blocks to provide a roof for the pump housing and a base for the fountain ornament. If the fountain sculpture is very heavy, it may need bolting on to

the concrete blocks, in which case the pool may need to be temporarily drained to mortar the blocks on to the fibreglass bottom. The sculpture can be bolted to the blocks once the mortar is hard.

10. Lead the pump cable through the pump housing and over the side of the pool to a waterproof junction box at the side.

11. When satisfied with the rigidity of the fountain fill the pool to the finished water level. Adjust the height of the fountain spray using the regulating valve supplied with the pump kit.

Log slice fountain

Size: 1.2m (4ft) across and high

Materials

9 log slices increasing in
  diameter from 15cm (6in)
  to 60cm (2ft) ranging in
  thickness from 7cm (3in)
  to 15cm (6in)
8 spacer slices of the same timber
  13mm (1.2in) thick and
  7–22cm (3–9in) in diameter
Circular pre-formed rigid fibreglass pool 45cm (18in) deep
  and 1.2m (4ft) in diameter
Submersible pump
1.5m (5ft) rigid plastic or PVC
  pipe 13mm (½in) in diameter
60–90cm (2–3ft) flexible pipe
  13mm (½in) in diameter
Push-on plastic elbow joint to fit
  piping
Adjustable (gate) valve
8 hollow-centred concrete
  walling blocks 45 x 22 x
  10cm (18 x 19 x 4in)
1 x 25kg bag of ready-mixed
  mortar
1 x 3 litre tin of hardcoat
  polyurethane or yacht varnish
3 x 25kg bags of builder's sand
1 large tube of brown mastic
  sealant

Ornamental fountains are most commonly made of stone or metal and usually fit most effectively into a formal or urban environment. This unusual creation, however, is of a distinctly different character, modern in the boldness and asymmetry of its design yet innately rustic and timeless. The whole slices of tree trunk have a solid, tactile appeal and would look good in an rural setting, even in the corner of the tiniest cottage garden.

What will make or break the success of this fountain is the wood itself. Oak, ash or elm would all be a good choice of wood, but it is vital that the slices are well seasoned or natural ageing combined with the constant exposure to water and weather will split and warp the wood despite the protective layers of varnish. Suitable wood will not be cheap and it may take some time to track down a supplier.

Construction

1. Mark out the site for the pool by placing it upside down and marking the outline with a line of sand 2–5cm (1–2in) outside the pool's rim.
2. Dig out the pool area to a depth of 52cm (21in), which is 7cm (3in) deeper than the pool unit.
3. Spread a layer of sand 7cm (3in) deep over the bottom of the hole and rake level.
4. Insert the pool unit and check that it is level by placing a spirit level on top of a straight-edge long enough to straddle the pool. If necessary, remove the pool unit and adjust the level of sand.

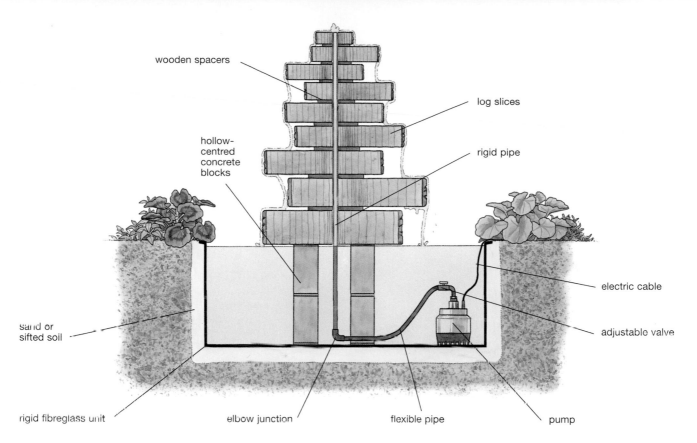

wooden spacers

log slices

hollow-centred concrete blocks

rigid pipe

sand or sifted soil

electric cable

adjustable valve

rigid fibreglass unit

elbow junction

flexible pipe

pump

5. Fill the pool with a little water to stabilize it and backfill around the outsides with sand or sifted soil, tamping down firmly with a thick stick. Empty out the water.

6. Mix the ready-mixed mortar to a stiff consistency. In the middle of the pool build two piers of concrete blocks about 15cm (6in) apart, each two blocks high and wide and laying the blocks on their wider sides. Mortar the blocks to the bottom of the pool as well as in between the courses.

7. Drill a hole through the centre of each of the wooden spacers and through the largest and smallest log slices. Drill a hole off-centre through the remaining log slices. The holes should be large enough to enable the slices to be threaded

on to the rigid pipe later.

8. Apply a coat of polyurethane with a cloth over the uppermost surfaces of the log slices and then apply 4–5 coats of varnish or polyurethane to all the exposed surfaces of timber.

9. Place the largest log slice on the concrete piers and after checking it is level secure with mastic to the piers. Push the rigid pipe through the centre hole so that there is 38cm (15in) of pipe emerging below the wood. Check that the pipe is vertical and then seal around it with mastic sealant.

10. Slide the largest spacer down the pipe on to the base log slice and seal between the wood and the pipe with mastic. Repeat, alternating log slices and spacers, working in

descending order of size and sealing each slice to the pipe with mastic until the top is reached. Check periodically that the rigid pipe is still vertical.

11. When the top log slice is in position, cut off any exposed pipe with a hacksaw so that the top of the pipe is flush with the timber.

12. Attach the elbow joint to the bottom of the rigid pipe and connect it to a flexible pipe from the outlet of the pump. Fit the adjustable valve to the flexible pipe.

13. Place the pump so that the adjustable valve is accessible from the poolside. Connect the pump's electric cable to a waterproof junction box

14. Fill the pool with water and disguise the sides with planting.

CONTAINERS

Imagination plays an important role in container water gardening. Here an old stone sink serves as a reservoir, surrounded by lush planting.

For some years now, I have kept a large, water-filled terracotta saucer (of the sort made to be placed under flowerpots) on the corner of the terrace. A shapely rock serves as a sundeck for all the birdlife in the neighbourhood that has discovered this simple bathing pool. It's planted round with variegated mints, periwinkle and ivy, and it is hugely entertaining to watch the antics of the little birds as they jostle each other for swimming rights. What could be simpler than this tiny container, yet it is undoubtedly a water feature.

General garden centres and water garden specialists stock a wide range of containers suitable for creating water features that can be used in any setting, from the smallest town garden to a featured aspect of a large garden. The choice of style and material will depend upon the style of garden; formal gardens and oriental style gardens would be best matched by a stone or *faux*-lead cistern; informal gardens would be complemented by wooden half-barrels, sinks and troughs and other found-object containers – let your creative imagination go. Glazed ceramic pots and bowls, like the vast Chinese ginger jars that are now widely available, or large terracotta urns and Ali Baba-style pots would also be suitable. Rather than just limiting the feature to one container, they could be used as a collection, each one planted individually with a single species of water plant, or plant up some and simply fill others with smooth rocks or use to house goldfish. Bowls can be arranged in a staggered stack to make a waterfall effect, with water overflowing from one bowl into the one below.

Whatever container you choose, inspect it carefully. Look out for cracks or faults in the glaze, splits or knots in wood, rust in metal. Make sure that barrel staves and hoops are sound and well-fitted. Once wet through, the wood in a barrel will swell to take up any slight degree of slackness, but you may need to seal or line it to make it entirely watertight – see pages 98–9.

Choose a site that is sheltered and receives shade for at least part of the day. Shallow water in barrels and other containers will warm up quickly, so fish and plants will appreciate shade during the hottest part of the day. Similarly, shallow water in containers will freeze easily, so some shelter and a relatively warm site near the house would be of benefit in areas where winter can be harsh.

When filling a container, rainwater is preferable to tap water, so it is advisable to collect rainwater (you should be doing this anyway) to top up the levels. In areas of hard water, the lime content of tap water can leave the familiar flaky white deposit you find in your kettle around the rim of the container. Should this happen it can be scrubbed off using descaler, but this is a performance best avoided in the first place.

Container water gardens require a little more attention than other water features to be kept looking their best. Water will evaporate more quickly than from a larger pool and plants will need to be kept under stricter control: 'Oh, look! Someone's tossed that old tub in the corner and it's filled with water and rubbish' is not the kind of response you wish to elicit!

When planting up, check carefully on the eventual size of plants you would like to grow. Many water plants spread fast in a season, so in such a restricted growing space ensure you choose dwarf forms, such as the pygmy water lilies *Nymphaea pygmaea* 'Helvola' and 'Rubra' and the miniature reedmace, *Typha minima*.

Containers also make excellent bog gardens for growing moisture-loving plants. Ensure that the container has three or four drainage holes (to prevent the moist soil from becoming stagnant) and fill it with moisture-retentive compost. You could, of course, have one of each type of container garden: one water, one bog. Complemented by container-grown Japanese maples or other small highly ornamental trees and shrubs this would make a very pretty and effective miniature water garden.

A collection of containers of similar shape can be combined to form a strikingly different 'waterfall' or rill feature.

Half-barrel

Size: approximately 60cm (2ft) in diameter

Materials

Half-barrel

2sq m (sq yd) flexible liner

1m (3ft) dark-coloured
wooden battening

About 2 bucketfuls of soft
sand or sifted soil

Waterproof sealant (if not
using flexible liner)

Blocks or bricks to support
planting baskets

Half-barrels are enormously popular for use as container gardens, and by their very nature lend themselves to water gardening. They can be set free-standing on a stable and level base or platform, or else, as in this case, sunk into the ground. This treatment provides more protection for the barrel and its contents, helping to keep the water cool during summer and insulating it to some degree from winter cold. However, if you choose to sink your barrel into the ground be sure to position it well off the main path so that you or your visitors will not stub toes or trip over the protruding rim. A free-standing half-barrel is more versatile as it can be emptied and moved to other parts of the garden with relative ease.

When buying a half-barrel, you may be lucky enough to pick a barrel in which the timbers will swell when the barrel is filled and become watertight without having to add a lining on the inside. Where this is possible it is advisable to paint the inside with a sealant which, in addition to keeping in the water, will also prevent any leaching of toxic chemicals which have been absorbed into the timber over the years when the barrel was in commercial use.

Topdressing the surrounding soil with gravel and cobbles creates more impact than if the barrel is sunk into an ordinary soil border. Where the barrel remains totally above ground level, provide a paving base to prevent any slight sinking which could affect the water level. Surrounding the base of the barrel with large decorative cobbles increases the impact in the same way as the gravel surround for the sunken barrel.

Construction

1. Mark out the position of the barrel by turning it upside down and inscribing its outline with sand.
2. As the barrel will sit on a layer of sand 5–7cm (2–3in) deep, the depth of the hole should be the same as the height of the barrel to

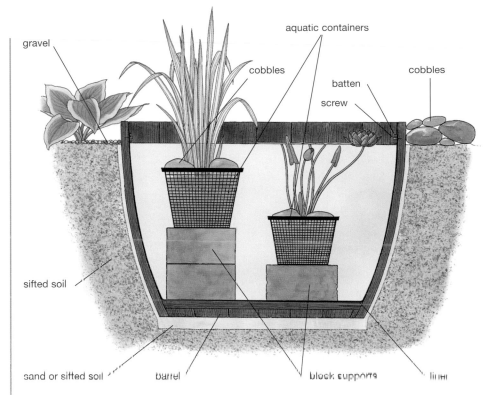

gravel — aquatic containers — cobbles — batten — cobbles — screw — sifted soil — sand or sifted soil — barrel — block supports — liner

allow the top of the barrel to be 5–7cm (2–3in) above ground level.
3. From 5cm (2in) outside the outline of sand, dig a hole to the same depth as the barrel.
4. Place a layer of sand 5–7cm (2–3in) on the bottom of the hole and spread out evenly and as level as possible.
5. Lift the barrel into the hole and check that it is level by placing a straight-edged piece of timber across the sides with a spirit level held on top.
6. Backfill with sifted soil around the sides.
7. Either seal the barrel inside with several coats of waterproof sealant

or line it with a piece of flexible liner. Fit the liner into the barrel, firming and folding the pleats of liner as neatly as possible.
8. Add water to within 7cm (3in) of the top of the barrel and trim off the surplus liner at the top. Fold the top 2–3cm (1in) of the liner against the side of the barrel and secure the fold with small pieces of batten just above the water line. Attach the battening with screws every 10–15cm (4–6in).
9. To provide different depths of planting for marginal plants and something such as a miniature waterlily, place bricks or small blocks under the planting baskets.

Brimming urn

Size: 75cm (30in) high

Materials

Suitable urn

Walling blocks or bricks for plinth

1 x 40kg (100lb) bag of ready-mixed mortar

Waterproof sealant

1m (3ft) copper pipe 13mm (½in) in diameter

Water tank pipe coupler

Submersible pump

This urn is a noteworthy object in its own right, the pleasing shape and decoration having existed for centuries – some of the earliest examples of this style were found in burial mounds of the ancient civilization of Dilmun, modern Bahrain. Rising out of a small formal pool, constantly bathed with a glistening sheet of water, it possesses all the qualities of the best water feature. The raised decoration plays an important role, making mini-cascades and attracting your attention to the detail.

Several types of urn can be converted into brimming water pots, from large upright focal points like this one, to pitchers 'casually' lying on their sides, overspilling into a pool. Terracotta is susceptible to frost damage when full of water or saturated, so it may be wise to drain off in the winter.

The urn can be sited within an existing pool or be a free-standing feature, in which case it is installed on a sunken reservoir disguised by cobbles. The reservoir can be circular or square in outline, but for an urn this size it will need to have a minimum diameter of 90cm (36in) for the shallow area that holds the cobbles. The inner sump to hold the water and pump will need to be 30–45cm (12–18in) in diameter and 40cm (16in) deep. (If

installing a reservoir, follow the instructions for the Urban Cascade on pages 72–3.)

Construction

1. Select an urn which has a level rim so that the water falls evenly around its circumference.

2. Drain the pool.

3. Inscribe the outline of the urn base on to the pool bottom in order to build a square, box-like plinth of the right size to give strong support to the urn. The plinth can be made of bricks, walling stone or concrete blocks. If the lining to your pool is concrete, the plinth can be mortared directly on to the concrete base, but if the pool is constructed using a flexible liner, this should be protected by offcuts of liner or polythene before starting to mortar the base of the plinth to the pool bottom. The number of courses will depend on the depth of the pool but the plinth should be high enough to support the base of the urn at water level. Once the mortar has hardened, in 48 hours, the pool can be refilled.

4. Drill a hole in the bottom of the pot which is large enough to accept a water tank coupler suitable for 13mm (½in) copper pipe.

5. Paint the entire urn, both inside and out, with three coats of colourless waterproof sealant. This will prevent the water permeating the pot, allowing it to retain the colour of dry terracotta and assist with the smooth flow of water over the sides. Sealing also gives added frost protection to terracotta, which is more vulnerable to damage when the clay is wet. Allow each coat of sealant to dry before applying the next coat.

6. Install the pump in the base of the plinth and connect to a waterproof junction box connected to the mains.

7. The best method of creating an effective seal where the pipe from the pump enters the base of the urn is to fit a brass water tank coupler. Some urns designed as water features will come ready fitted, so that a simple connection to the pump is all that is necessary, or can

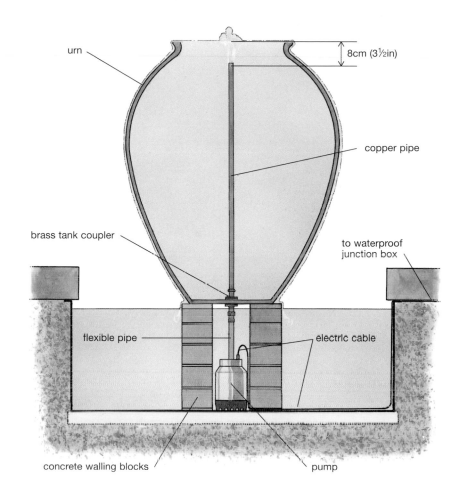

urn

8cm (3½in)

copper pipe

brass tank coupler

to waterproof junction box

flexible pipe

electric cable

concrete walling blocks

pump

be supplied with a conversion kit.

A tank coupler makes it easy to dismantle the pipework at any time in the future, but where this is unlikely to be necessary a simpler method is to insert a complete length of copper pipe through the base hole from just under the level of the top of the urn to a flexible pipe from the pump in the reservoir.

8. Drill the hole carefully with a slow-speed drill of the same size as the copper pipe. After this has been reamed out to allow the pipe to be pushed through the hole, seal the pipe to the urn with a mastic or silicone waterproofing compound. Apply this liberally and the seal should be good enough to prevent all but a slight seepage back into the pool.

9. Refill the pool and fill the urn. Adjust the flow of the pump to achieve a rate of spillage over the sides of the urn which is gentle and constant, without too much turbulence.

CREATIVE
planting

The many brightly coloured cultivars of the day lily can lift an otherwise green and leafy waterside planting. This is Hemerocallis *'Pink Damask' which blends prettily with the buff-grey foliage of* Macleaya cordata.

Unless your water feature is for purely architectural reasons, plants will probably be top of the agenda, and plant lovers, in particular those who can't resist a challenge, will welcome the opportunity provided by the special environments they are able to create: deep water for the incomparable beauty of waterlilies; boggy gardens for moisture-loving marginal plants; container water gardens for choice and treasured plants. One passionate gardener of my acquaintance has a half-barrel pool by his potting shed where he can keep a lovingly watchful eye on the soft green, velvety foliage of his tender water lettuce, *Pistia stratiotes.*

The temptation offered by the watery environment to grow as many kinds of water plant as possible is an alluring one. To succumb might lead to disaster, as anyone with an overstocked border can tell you. Aquatic plants are notorious colonizers and one or two plants may begin to crowd out the others and before you know it, the balance is gone and so is the pretty picture. While the range of water plants is rather more limited than the vast panoply of herbaceous border perennials, there is still a huge variety to choose from. Space will be limited in a small pool, but if you try to accommodate as many different types as possible the result will be in danger of becoming spotty and unharmonious – a little restraint will be worth it.

When considering which plants would be suitable, it is a good plan to seek out nurseries or departments of garden centres which specialize in aquatic and moisture-loving plants, because they are best able to give you sound advice about which plants will suit your conditions and purpose. Visit flower shows and other gardens, too, to glean ideas and see how plantings look at different times of the year.

Shape and colour

With the exception of waterlilies and a few moisture-loving
perennials, water plants and marginals are not generally known
for their flower colour; so the key to a successful plant grouping
lies in the contrasts of leaf size, shape and texture: multi-lobed,
palmate leaves like rodgersias, against entire oval leaves like
skunk cabbage *(Lysichiton americanus)*, against strappy, sword-
shaped leaves like flag iris. Imagine the smooth and glossy foliage
of bog arum *(Calla palustris)* against the deeply veined and
textured leaves of *Senecio smithii*; blue-green hostas against
bronzy-purple ligularia; the erect swords of the sweet rush, *Acorus
calamus*, rising up from the water to meet the airy, spreading dome of a
dwarf Japanese maple, *Acer palmatum*.

So many water plants have striking foliage that you could easily
compose an attractive show from just three sorts, for example: the
American arrowhead, *Sagittaria latifolia*, which takes its name from the
broad, flat, arrow shape of its soft green leaves; the grass-like dwarf
reedmace, *Typha minima*, and the glossy pads and perfectly formed blooms
of a small-flowered waterlily. If you are concentrating the planting in boggy
areas around the pool perimeter, use bold-leaved, moisture-loving plants
such as hostas, rodgersias and variegated iris to play up the reflective nature
of the water. The vertical leaves and stems of rushes and irises, rising
directly out of the water, will provide a striking contrast with an unbroken
sheet of water.

Bear in mind that your planting areas will be comparatively small, so
choose plants that will be in scale. That is not to say that you can't use one
or two really expansive plants, like the ornamental rhubarb, *Rheum
palmatum,* or the skunk cabbage as a specimen or eyecatcher around a
pond. The latter can be quite vigorous, and for small features it is in
general wise to avoid water-dwelling plants that will be invasive. The pretty

The pale variegation and striation of the
bamboo-like Sasa veitchii *and* Acorus
calamus *are complemented by the*
flowers of the elegant Viburnum
mariesii. *Pale colours seen in reflection*
on the water surface have a particularly
entrancing sparkle.

In a small formal raised pool like this the key is restraint. Limit the accompanying planting scheme to perhaps two or three plants, and reserve one especially stylish specimen for in-the-water growing.

The colour wheel.

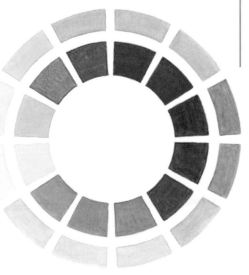

variegated *Houttuynia cordata* 'Chameleon' is one such plant that has to be used with discretion, and there are waterlilies that can quickly take over even a good-sized pond, so be sure to ascertain from the nursery that the ones you have chosen are dwarf or slow-growing.

Such flower colour as exists among the aquatic tribe tends to be fairly low-key – pale creams and yellows, forget-me-not blue and so on – with the main show in spring and early summer. Of course there are brighter colours, but these tend to be found among the marginal plants. Marsh marigolds, *Caltha palustris*, are shining, egg-yolk yellow; the species is single-flowered but the cultivar 'Flore Pleno' is splendidly double. The candelabra primulas, *Primula japonica*, are also brightly coloured, carrying their whorls of little flowers up tall, upright stems. Their shades of white, yellow, carmine and pink look well reflected in the still water of a small pool.

Colour can be used to enhance the mood of the water garden. Pale blue, ivory white, soft pastels – these are cool and soothing hues that can be incorporated to support a feeling of meditative calm around a reflecting pool or in an elegant formal fountain arrangement. Hot colours, those that fall in the red, orange and yellow part of the spectrum, are lively and cheerful and will make just that sort of contribution to an informal water garden display. Or use them with large leaves to create a tropical air around a small pool.

The importance of colour will depend on the style of pool and your individual taste – it could be argued that colour harmony around a wildlife pool is unimportant (although plants chosen to emphasize the pool's 'naturalness' are unlikely to present colour clashes), whereas the effect of a formal pool can be much influenced by the colour combinations around it.

Harmonizing colours can sometimes be difficult to achieve and understand, and it may be useful to refer to a colour wheel. Adjacent colours harmonize because they share a pigment, whereas opposite, or complementary, colours contrast or intensify each other. A simple colour wheel, of course, does not take into account tonal variations and the effects of light and shadow or texture, but it can be a useful starting point. Using foliage and white flowers will also break up any disharmonies.

Style

The simplicity and symmetry associated with formal design will be enhanced if this is followed through in the planting: a single stand of water iris will emphasize the formality where a riotous mixed planting might detract from the overall effect. A plain, even severe, setting provides the ideal frame for a single specimen planting, particularly if the clear water can provide a dramatic reflection. A decorative grass, such as the striped *Schoenoplectus lacustris* 'Zebrinus', the lizard's tail *(Saururus cernuus)* and, in a mild area, the cool spathes of arum lilies *(Zantedeschia aethiopica)*, all benefit from being shown off in this way. Cannas, so often misused as 'dot' plants in municipal beds, create a wonderfully exotic effect when plunged into deeper water for the summer (they will need to be retrieved and stored over winter like dahlias, for they are not very hardy). Formal pools do not necessarily require this amount of stark restraint, but it is much easier in a formal than an informal pool to over-emphasize the planting to the detriment of the pool itself.

This is not to say that, in an informal setting, anything goes. The trick here is not to lose sight of the point of the feature. For a wildlife pool, concentrate on a collection of plants akin to those that might be found around a local natural pool and do not be tempted to introduce something too alien, however enticing it may look at the garden centre. The aim should be one of quiet harmony, with no jarring, contradictory messages.

Where you have gone to the expense and effort of installing an interesting ornamental fountain or a decorative wall plaque, make sure that the impact of this is not lost among an exciting array of plants also shouting for attention. An unadorned water spout, on the other hand,

Tumbling roses and purple irises accent the simplicity and the medieval character of this tiny garden, where the cobble-edged sunken pool doubles as a moat, which needs to be crossed before reaching the small carpet of emerald grass beyond.

might need to be surrounded by a tangled mass of climbers to achieve the right effect. And in many situations it will be the planting that comes first, to be enhanced by the sight and sound of water.

Plants with a purpose

There are several categories of plants for water gardens, distinguished by their preferred growing conditions.

Deep-water aquatics have their roots at the bottom of the pool but their leaves resting on the surface. The role of the deep-water plants is a particularly important and beneficial one. They decorate the pool with some of the most exquisite flowers, and provide vital shade during the summer months. Fish and other aquatic creatures also enjoy this shade, particularly when herons are known to be regular visitors. When creating a planting plan for the pool, aim at covering between a third and a half of the water surface with leaves, with clumps of foliage separated by roughly equal distances of clear water to provide the best effect, as a pool dominated by too many surface leaves loses much of its impact.

The best-known and most popular deep-water plants are the waterlilies, with cultivars and species to suit nearly every size of water feature. But there are other deep-water plants, too, which give variety of foliage and

A pool with several depths of water will make it possible to grow a wide range of deep-water aquatics, which carry their leaves on the surface of the water but are rooted in the bottom of the pool. The leaves provide valuable shade in summer.

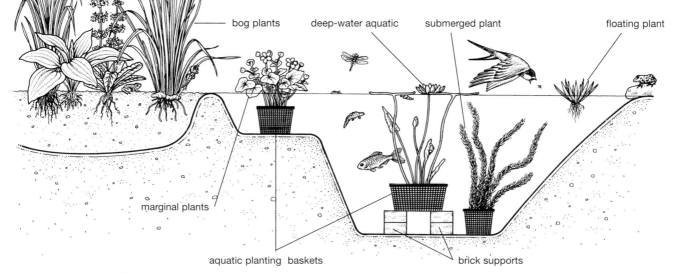

bog plants   deep-water aquatic   submerged plant   floating plant

marginal plants

aquatic planting baskets   brick supports

flower on the surface, from the dark strap-like leaves and strange scented flowers of the water hawthorn (*Aponogeton distachyos*) to the upright 'pokers' of golden club (*Orontium aquaticum*).

Submerged plants are also rooted in soil at the pool bottom, but have their leaves and stems entirely under water. They play an important role in oxygenating the water and compete with non-beneficial algae for sunlight and nutrients; without submerged oxygenators, a pool will soon choke with algae. Submerged plants also benefit fish by providing shade and shelter and by exchanging carbon dioxide for oxygen (see pages 31–2).

Floating plants are exactly the opposite to submerged plants: they too are useful in keeping the water healthy but they float on the surface with their roots trailing free in the water.

The decorative **marginals** grow in shallow water with most of their foliage above the water line – their wild relations are found growing on the shallow banks of rivers, natural ponds and lakes. They are treated in much the same way as ordinary herbaceous perennials except that their roots must be kept permanently wet. Their tolerance of depth of water varies and the depth suiting each species can be found in the Plant Catalogue on pages 118–22. In small water features they are best grown in aquatic planting baskets which prevents them from being too invasive and allows them to be moved around more easily.

Pools are often constructed with shelves at various depths running around the edge to provide growing positions for marginal plants; if your pool does not have this facility you can use brick or up-turned pot supports, but this is less satisfactory than making proper arrangements to begin with.

The final group of plants for the water garden are the **moisture-loving bog plants**. These are perennials, either herbaceous or evergreen, which revel in damp but not saturated conditions. If your garden has an area where the soil is by nature constantly moist, this could be the place to site a

Even the smallest water feature has room for one plant, but be sure to select one that will provide interest both before and after flowering – plants with pretty, variegated foliage are an obvious choice.

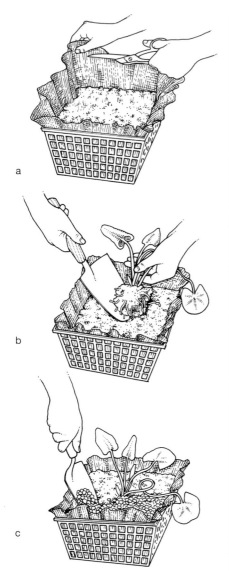

a

b

c

Before planting a waterlily, line the basket with hessian. Half fill the lined basket with soil or a mixture of soil and compost (a) and plant the waterlily in the soil (b). Add more soil, then cover the surface of the growing medium with a layer of pea gravel so that the soil does not wash away (c).

water feature (but beware of 'hippoing' – see page 21) and then exploit the natural conditions by developing a collection of bog plants. Alternatively, a boggy area can be created artificially beside the pool (see pages 28–9).

The Plant Catalogue beginning on page 110 gives further planting and growing details for each of these types of plant, and recommends the most suitable for small water gardens.

Growing conditions

Water-bound plants are largely reliant on the conditions provided for them, so the soil and nutrients you supply are particularly important.

Soil can be put directly into the bottom of a pool and the plants rooted into the mix and then the soil surface 'mulched' or covered with a layer of washed pebbles. If this seems too much like making mud-pies it also has several disadvantages: although heavy garden soil can be used in pools, sandy or peaty soil should be avoided, as should any garden soil which may have been dressed with fertilizers or chemicals. These may leach out into the water later and either cause excessive clouding or prove toxic to plants or fish. Use proprietary aquatic composts, available at aquatic nurseries and most garden centres, if there is the slightest doubt as to the suitability of the garden soil.

The most convenient method of planting is to use special aquatic baskets, which have mesh sides to allow the exchange of gases. Line baskets with large-mesh sides with a permeable lining such as a square of hessian to prevent the soil from oozing out of the sides. (There is no need to line the more expensive planting baskets, which have a very fine-mesh or louvre sides.)

A containerized plant will have its growth inhibited so that any invasive tendencies can be curbed, at least for a time, and a plant in a basket is also easier to move around if you want to change the arrangement or clean out the pool.

It is always worth checking the pH of any growing medium so that you can ensure that you are providing plants with the conditions they prefer. Kits are available for testing water pH; the higher the reading, the more alkaline it becomes; a reading of 5.5 to 6.5 is neutral and below that progressively more acid. Chemical additives can be used to correct the pH and obtain a neutral condition.

If you have purchased your plants by mail order, submerge the roots in a bucket of water for several hours to give them a good drink; most can remain this way for a few days until you get around to planting them.

Before planting, firm the soil very thoroughly into the containers. As soon as the containers are submerged, the air is dispelled and the soil sinks in the container. Baskets which have only been lightly filled will be only half full after a short period under water. Topdress with a layer of pea shingle to stop the soil from floating away. If you plan to have fish, particularly carp, in your pool, make the topdressing at least 2–3cm (1in) thick as bottom-feeding fish tend to forage around the soil in the containers and disturb the soil.

Any additional fertilizer added to the compost to help plants establish quickly should be of the slow-release type. Ordinary fertilizers would quickly dissolve and release salts into the water causing a rapid surge of green algae growth. Slow-release fertilizers can be bought in tablet or sachet form and pushed into the compost at the same time as planting.

Freshly planted waterlilies and other deep-water aquatics should not be placed directly on to the pool bottom but placed on a pier of bricks or upturned clay pots, so that the young plant is no more than 15cm (6in) below the water surface. As the plant grows the bricks are gradually removed layer by layer, or the pots replaced by smaller ones, until the plant is strong enough to reach the surface when the container is on the pool bottom.

For most water gardeners the ideal plant is the waterlily. Small water gardens can be graced with this lovely flower if the choice is carefully made, selecting varieties that are not invasive and dwarf in habit. 'Perry's Pink' is ideal for small pools and ponds.

PLANT
Catalogue

DEEP-WATER PLANTS

With their roots in the deeper regions of the pond and their leaves reaching up to the surface, these plants prefer ample water depth over their crowns, ranging from 22cm (9in) for the dwarfer species to as much as 1m (3ft) for the very vigorous ones. Deep-water plants are dominated by the waterlilies but there is an interesting selection of alternative plants to give variety of leaf shape and flower.

New plants should be purchased in late spring just as growth has started. Avoid disturbing plants in the winter in case any cut or damaged root begins to rot in the cold water; any damage will heal quickly when the plant is in active growth. Deep-water plants are frequently sold bare-rooted, having been freshly divided from the parent plant. Buying containerized plants saves root disturbance, but

established aquatic plants in containers are heavy and the extra expense is seldom justified as bare-rooted plants soon catch up in growth if planted at the right time. As deep-water plants require good root systems so that nutrient reserves support the plant to reach the surface, the largest size of planting basket should be used. These are 40cm (16in) in diameter by 20cm (8in) deep and take 30 litres of aquatic compost to fill.

The planting depth (**PD**) for deep-water plants refers to the depth of water above the growing point, and not the depth of the pool. The spread (**S**) refers to the average area which the leaves will cover, although in small planting containers they may not achieve this. (**H**) refers to a plant's expected height.

Aponogeton distachyos
(Water hawthorn, Cape pondweed)
Perennial with oblong, bright green

leaves up to 20cm (8in) long by 8cm (3in) wide that are almost evergreen in mild winters. A tolerant plant, it provides a change from the circular pads of waterlilies. The strongly scented white flowers are produced in spring, often providing a second flush in the autumn when the waterlilies are over and the water is cooler. For this reason it is recommended for pools where there is inadequate sunshine for the successful flowering of waterlilies. The very distinctive flowers are 10cm (4in) long, white with purple-brown anthers and held above the surface. **PD** up to 60cm (2ft). **S** 1.2m (4ft). Frost hardy in temperate areas. Sun or shade.

Hydrocharis morsus ranae
(Frogbit)
Perennial with runners forming new plants with rosettes of kidney-shaped, shiny green leaves 2–3cm (1in) across. The papery white

flowers have 3 petals with a yellow centre 2cm (¾in) across. They form a home and shade for colonies of life in shallow warm areas of wildlife pools where roots can form in mud. They are rather vulnerable to snail damage.
PD up to 30cm (12in).
S Indefinite. Hardy. Sun.

Nuphar japonica
(Japanese pond lily)
Perennial with narrow oval surface leaves 40cm (16in) long and 12cm (5in) wide, and submerged, wavy, heart-shaped leaves that are a little smaller than the surface leaves. The round yellow flowers held just above the surface in summer are 5cm (2in) in diameter. Although more tolerant of deeper water and shade than most waterlilies, the Japanese pond lily requires more sun for optimum flower production than its more vigorous relatives, *Nuphar advena* (American spatterdock) and *Nuphar lutea* (Common pond lily).
PD 30cm (12in). **S** 3ft (1m). Hardy. Sun.

Orontium aquaticum
(Golden club)
Deciduous perennial with bluish-green leaves with a silvery sheen on the underside. The poker-like yellow flowerheads on white stalks stand well above the water.
PD to 30cm (12in). **S** 24in (60cm). Hardy. Sun.

Polygonum amphibium
(Willow grass, amphibious bistort)
Perennial with long-stalked floating leaves 7–10cm (3–4in) long and 2–4cm (1–1½in) wide, borne on stems 30–90cm (12–36in) long which root from the stems. The densely packed pink flowers are borne on spikes 5cm (2in) above the water in mid summer. A useful and attractive plant for wildlife pools.
PD up to 45cm. **S** Indefinite. (18in). Hardy. Full sun.

WATERLILIES

Epitomizing the water garden with their distinctive flowers and leaves, these beautiful flowers change shape and colour each day, their leaves providing vital shade to the submerged world. All the waterlilies bear the generic name of *Nymphaea*, and the waterlily family is one of the oldest families of water and marsh plants scattered widely around the world. For cultivation purposes they are split into two main groups, the hardies and the tropicals, although this selection only includes the hardies, which are able to withstand the water freezing over in the winter. The flowers vary in size, but generally are always in proportion to the leaf, ranging from 2–3cm (1in) in the pygmy varieties to 30cm (12in) in some of the tropicals.

Waterlilies are sold as either container-grown or bare-rooted plants which have been freshly removed from the parent plant. The bare-rooted plants should never be allowed to dry out before planting and they should be planted as soon as possible into aquatic baskets. The size of the container will relate to the vigour of the plant: most waterlilies will need large baskets, but the dwarf varieties will need no more than a medium-sized basket. Rich fibrous garden soil or aquatic planting compost is required for most waterlilies as they are gross feeders. Supplement this with a slow-release fertilizer.

Plant the roots on to firmed compost in the aquatic container which is filled to about three-quarters full. Cover with more soil and firm the root so that the growing point is just at the surface of the soil. Topdress the container with pea shingle and it is ready for immersing.

There are waterlilies suitable for every size of pond from barrels and tubs to large pools. Aim at having sufficient cover of leaves to cover about a half to two-thirds of the water surface once they have grown. The selection below is grouped into the main colour shades.

White

'Caroliniana Nivea'
Almost round leaves 20–25cm (8–10in) across and star-shaped, fragrant flowers 12–15cm (5–6in) in diameter with yellow stamens. Best in a large container where it can form an adequate root.
PD 30–60cm (1–2ft).
S 1.2–1.5m (4–5ft).

'Gonnere'
Slightly bronzed young leaves mature to round green leaves 15–22cm (6–9in) in diameter. The globe-shaped fragrant flower is 10–15cm (4–6in) in diameter with yellow stamens. An ideal cultivar for all sized pools, this snowball-like flower stays open late in the day.
PD 30–45cm (12–18in).
S 1–1.2m. (3–4ft).

'Marliacea Albida'
Slightly bronzed young leaves mature to round green leaves 22cm (9in) in diameter. The cup-shaped flowers are 12–15cm (5–6in) in diameter with yellow stamens. A good free-flowering cultivar suitable for pools with a limited spread.
PD 30–45cm (12–18in).
S 1–1.2m (3–4ft).

'Virginalis'
Purple or bronzed young leaves mature to round green leaves 22cm (9in) in diameter. The cup-shaped fragrant flowers are 10–15cm (4–6in) in diameter with yellow stamens. One of the best whites which is free flowering and reliable.
PD 38–45cm (15–18in).
S 1–1.2m (3–4ft).

Reds

'Escarboucle'
Brown-tinged young leaves mature to round green leaves 25–28cm (10–11in) in diameter. The cup-shaped flowers become star-shaped about 15–17cm (6–7in) in diameter in a bright vermilion red with outer petals tipped white and deep orange stamens. One of the best reds which stays open later in the afternoon than most other red varieties.
PD 30–60cm (1–2ft).
S 1.2–1.5m (4–5ft).

'Froebelii'
Bronzed young leaves mature to round, pale green leaves 15cm (6in)

in diameter. The cup-shaped burgundy red flowers become star-shaped 10–12cm (4–5in) across with orange-red stamens. An excellent waterlily for barrels or small pools which will thrive in cold water better than most. **PD** 15–30cm (6–12in). **S** 1m (3ft).

'James Brydon'
Purplish brown young leaves blotched with dark purple mature to round green leaves 17cm (7in) in diameter. The cup-shaped, brilliant rose-red flowers are 10–12cm (4–5in) in diameter with orange-red stamens. A very popular variety for barrels or medium-sized pools for its shape of flower and free-flowering habit.
PD 30–45cm (12–18in).
S 1–1.2m (3–4ft).

'Laydekeri Fulgens'
Purplish-green young leaves, blotched with dark purple, mature to round green leaves 17–20cm (7–8in) in diameter. The cup-shaped, burgundy-red flowers are 12–15cm (5–6in) in diameter with

orange red stamens. One of the first to bloom in spring, this free-flowering variety is suitable for all sized pools.
PD 30–45cm (12–18in).
S 1.2–1.5m (4–5ft).

'Lucida'
The mature oval leaves are speckled with large purple blotches and grow to 25cm (10in) long and 22cm (9in) wide. The star-shaped flowers have red inner petals and whitish pink outer petals with pink veins 12–15cm (5–6in) in diameter with yellow stamens. Free-flowering with attractive leaves, it is suitable for any sized pool.
PD 30–45cm (12–18in).
S 1.2–1.5m (4–5ft).

'Vesuve'
The almost circular green leaves are 22–25cm (9–10in) across. The fragrant flowers are star-shaped and glowing red, deepening with age, 17cm (7in) in diameter with inward-pointing petals and orange stamens. It has a long blooming season in addition to opening early

in the morning and closing late in the afternoon.
PD 30–45cm (12–18in).
S 1.2m (4ft).

Pinks
'Firecrest'
Deep purple young leaves mature to round green leaves 22cm (9in) in diameter. The star-shaped, lavender-pink flowers which are held slightly above the water are 15cm (6in) in diameter with inner stamens orange and outer stamens pink.
PD 30–45cm (12–18in).
S 1.2m (4ft).

'Marliacea Carnea'
Purplish young leaves mature to oval, deep green leaves 17–20cm (7–8in) long. The light pink flowers are 10–12cm (4–5in) in diameter with yellow stamens. A good pink for medium-sized pools.
PD 30–45cm (12–18in).
S 1.2–1.5m (4–5ft).

'Pearl of the Pool'
Bronzed young leaves mature to round green leaves 25cm (10in) in

diameter. The star-shaped, fragrant pink flowers are 12–15cm (5–6in) in diameter with pinkish orange stamens. Plant in a large container.
PD 30–45cm (12–18in).
S 1.2–1.5m (4–5ft).

'Pink Sensation'
Purplish young leaves mature to round green leaves up to 25cm (10in) in diameter. The cup-shaped flowers become star-shaped 12–15cm (5–6in) in diameter with yellow inner stamens and pink outer ones. One of the best pinks, whose flowers stay open late into the afternoon.
PD 30–45cm (12–18in).
S 1.2m (4ft).

Yellows
'Helvola'
Oval, heavily mottled, purple-blotched leaves 12cm (5in) long and 10cm (4in) wide with purple undersides. The slightly fragrant flowers are cup-shaped, later becoming star-shaped 5–7cm (2–3in) in diameter with yellow stamens. This small waterlily makes

a perfect subject for a barrel.
PD 15–22cm (6–9in).
S 60cm (24in).

'Marliacea Chromatella'

Coppery young leaves with purple streaks mature to purple, mottled mid-green leaves 15–20cm (6–8in) in diameter. The free-flowering canary yellow flowers are 15cm (6in) in diameter with broad, incurved petals and golden stamens. One of the best and most reliable yellow waterlilies.
PD 30–45cm (12–18in).
S 1.2–1.5m (4–5ft).

'Sulphurea Grandiflora'
Speckled purple blotched young leaves mature to oval green leaves 25cm (10in) long. The cup-shaped, sweet-smelling flowers held slightly above the water become star-shaped

later, 15–17cm (6–7in) across with yellow stamens.
PD 30–45cm (12–18in).
S 1–1.2m (3–4ft).

Changeable
'Aurora'
Olive green leaves 15cm (6in) across with many small red-purple mottles. The free-flowering cup-shaped, later star-shaped, semi-double flowers are 5cm (2in) across. They are slightly scented, cream in bud opening to yellow, then passing through orange to a slightly flecked blood red with glowing golden orange stamens.
PD 30–45cm (12–18in).
S 75cm (30in).

SUBMERGED PLANTS

These plants, commonly referred to as 'oxygenators', resemble water weeds and are valued, not for their ornamental attraction, but for the major contribution they make towards clear water. Although there may be a natural pond in the area, raiding this for water weed is not only destroying a natural balance and habitat in the wild but the plants may well introduce unwanted micro-organisms to the new ornamental pond. The oxygenators sold by good aquatic nurseries will have been grown in hygienic conditions and should be free of snail eggs, disease spores and other fry.

Oxygenators are sold from spring to autumn, and aquatic centres generally have a selection of approximately six different species. It is advisable to buy a selection of species as some will grow better than others in different conditions, and some, like the autumn starwort (*Callitriche autumnalis*), remain in growth well into the winter.

As soon as the plants are available, remove the bunches from the waterproof bags and store them in buckets of water until they are planted. Use medium-sized aquatic planting baskets, planting five bunches to each container, one in the centre and one in each corner. Insert the bunches of oxygenator into the soil with a dibber, burying about 2–3in (1in) of the basal stems. The bunches have a clasp or tie at the base which should be buried to prevent the risk of the bunches floating if inadequately firmed in. After firming around each bunch, topdress the soil with a thin layer of pea shingle to prevent the soil from floating as the container is submerged. Place the baskets gently on the bottom of the pool.

A rough guide to the number of oxygenators initially required is one bunch to every sq. ft or 10 bunches to every sq. metre of water surface. So a pool 3 x 2m (10 x 6ft) will need 60 bunches in 12 containers. As they become established they can be easily thinned in small pools before becoming invasive. They should also be trimmed back if they get straggly.

Callitriche hermaphroditica, syn. *C. autumnalis* (Autumn starwort)
Perennial with thin branching stems up to 20in (50cm) long with small narrow light green leaves. It is an excellent oxygenator and refuge for freshwater fleas, shrimps and fish fry which need good supplies of oxygen. Unlike most starworts it does not develop surface rosettes and grows mainly near pool bottoms.
S indefinite. Hardy. Full sun.

Ceratophyllum demersum (Hornwort)
Perennial with slender, often rootless stems growing to 30–60cm (1–2ft) long, supporting whorls of brittle, dark green, forked leaves 1–4cm (½–1½in) long which become denser near the growing point. It is tolerant of shade and will grow in deeper water than most other submerged aquatics. It makes an excellent oxygenator and refuge for fish fry, tolerating a wide range of water conditions
Up to 60cm (2ft) of water.
S indefinite. Hardy. Sun or shade.

Fontinalis antipyretica (Water moss)
Evergreen perennial moss with round or triangular branched stems

up to 20–25cm (8–10in) and olive green moss-like leaves which grow directly from the stem and overlap each other like scales. Grow in full light in shallow water weighing the plants on to boulders where they form a dense carpet which acts as a good oxygenator. Excellent in moving water.

Up to 18in of water. **S** indefinite. Hardy. Sun or shade.

Hottonia palustris (Water violet)
An attractive oxygenator bearing both decorative foliage and aerial flowers, this hardy perennial produces stolons and erect stems which bear whorls of deeply divided, light green leaves up to 13cm (5in) long. Erect spikes 30–40cm (12–16in) long emerge above the water in spring bearing pale lilac flowers 2–3cm (1in) across. They are not easy to establish and perform best in shallow, clear, mud-bottomed pools rather than in planting baskets.
H 30–90cm (1–3ft). Up to 45cm (18in) of water. **S** indefinite. Hardy. Sun or shade.

Lagarosiphon major, syn. *Elodea crispa* (Curly water thyme)
Semi-evergreen perennial with branched fragile stems up to 1m (3ft) long covered in tiny, thin, curling leaves, 0.6–2.5cm (¼in–1in) wide. Used extensively as an oxygenator, it forms dense submerged masses of branched stems which should be cut back every autumn.
Up to 1m (3ft) of water.
S indefinite. Hardy. Full sun.

Myriophyllum verticillatum (Milfoil, myriad leaf)
Perennial with spreading stems 1m (3ft) long and tightly packed needle-like bright green leaves in whorls. The inconspicuous yellowish flowers are borne on a spike up to 15cm (6in) tall just above the water surface in summer. The delicate leaves create excellent homes for fish fry as well as oxygenating the water. Often amphibious, it makes a good subject for softening shallow edges.
Up to 45cm (18in) of water.
S indefinite. Half-hardy 1°C (34°F) min. temp. Sun or shade.

Potamogeton crispus (Curled pondweed)
Perennial with long cylindrical stems bearing narrow, almost translucent leaves 10cm (4in) long with wavy edges when mature. The small crimson and creamy white flowers emerge just above the water surface in summer. Forming a home for fish fry and numerous submerged organisms, they spread rapidly in mud-bottomed pools and will tolerate cloudy or shady water better than any other oxygenator.
Up to 1m (3ft) of water. **H** and **S** indefinite. Hardy. Sun or shade.

Ranunculus aquatilis (Water crowfoot)
Annual or perennial with deeply lobed, kidney-shaped floating leaves up to 8cm (3in) long. The small, buttercup-shaped flowers held above the water are white with a yellow base to the petals. They are best at a depth of 15–60cm (6–24in) where they can root in a mud bottom.
Up to 1m (3ft) of water. **H** and **S** indefinite. Hardy. Sun or shade.

FLOATING PLANTS

Floaters, whether hardy or tender, are particularly appropriate to small water features as they can easily be kept in check. They can make a dramatic impact on water clarity quite quickly if they almost cover the water surface in the early days. The floaters, like the oxygenators, feed on the mineral salts in the water through their fine root hairs which drape into the water. The fine roots of some species also make ideal refuges for fish fry.

Most types of hardy floating plants have very small leaves and are sold by the bunch in plastic bags. Planting simply involves sprinkling the bunch on to the water surface.

There are also larger floating plants which are not hardy – the two mostly commonly available are the water hyacinth *(Eichhornia crassipes)* and the water lettuce *(Pistia stratiotes)*. No matter where these are placed initially, any wind will move them around on the water, as they have more upright and larger leaves than the hardy floaters. These will require overwintering indoors on wet mud or in a large frost-free aquarium partially filled with water and kept in full light.

Azolla caroliniana
(Fairy moss, water fern)
A small perennial fern that forms clusters of soft, pale green leaves which turn purplish red in the autumn. Each leaf is attached to a single fine root. It can be invasive so thin regularly.
S indefinite. Slightly tender. Full sun.

Eichhornia crassipes
(Water hyacinth)
Evergreen or semi-evergreen floater which forms clumps of buoyant foliage on spongy swollen stalks. In warm summers it produces pale blue hyacinth-like flowers up to 15–22cm (6–9in) high. It may root in any mud in shallow water.
H 22–30cm (9–12in). **S** indefinite. Tender. Full sun.

Pistia stratiotes (Water lettuce)
A deciduous floating aquatic which is evergreen in warm climates where the minimum temperature is no less than 10°C (50°F). The overlapping pale green leaves which resemble a lettuce in their arrangement are velvety, and whitish green on the undersides. Keep thinning new plants in the summer.
H 22–30cm (9–12in). **S** indefinite. Tender. Full sun.

Salvinia auriculata (Butterfly fern)
A floating fern which is evergreen in warm climates where the mimimum temperature falls no lower than 10°C (50°F). The pale green or purplish brown leaves are tightly arranged on branched stems and covered in silky hairs.
H 2–3cm (1in). **S** indefinite. Tender. Full sun.

MARGINAL PLANTS

In addition to forming a decorative margin in the shallower water, marginal plants also help to achieve clear water by removing excess nutrients through their roots.

Marginals are available bare-rooted or ready planted in containers (although they may need transplanting to a larger one). Plant them in medium-sized or large aquatic containers, using good-quality aquatic soil and putting the growing point at soil level, as with an ordinary herbaceous perennial. Firm down well and cover the soil's surface with pea gravel before placing in the shallow water or on the marginal shelf of a deeper pool.

Provided the plants are containerized, the following selection is suitable for small–medium pools. After each plant is listed its expected height (**H**), spread in a container (**S**) and tolerance of water depth (**PD**).

Acorus calamus 'Variegatus'
(Myrtle flag, sweet flag)
Deciduous perennial with a spreading habit and distinctive iris-like erect mid green leaves with a cream striped variegation and occasional areas of wrinkling along the edges. The unusual flower resembles a small horn emerging laterally just below the tip of a leaf. It makes a striking impact among the edges of a wildlife pool.
H 75cm (30in). **S** 60cm (24in).
PD no deeper than 22cm (9in).
Hardy. Full sun.

Alisma plantago-aquatica
(Water plantain)
Deciduous perennial with rosettes of oval, semi-upright leaves with long leaf stalks emerging above the water. The flower spike contains numerous small, pinky white flowers in summer. The seeds, which tend to set easily in the surrounding wet soil, are a valuable food supply for birds.
H 75cm (30in). **S** 45 cm (18in).
PD no deeper than 25cm (10in).
Hardy. Full sun.

Calla palustris (Bog arum)
Deciduous or semi-evergreen perennial with a long, conspicuous creeping surface root and round to heart-shaped, glossy, mid to dark green, pointed leaves that are firm and leathery. The flowers appear in spring, resembling small flattened arum lilies, followed by clusters of red or orange berries.
H 25cm (10in). **S** 30cm (12in).
PD no more than 5cm (2in).
Hardy. Full sun.

Eriophorum angustifolium
(Cotton grass)
Evergreen perennial, a marsh or marginal aquatic with a long root-stock. The short, angled stems bear grooved, grass-like, flat leaves. The conspicuous tassel-like flowers are white and downy in cotton-like tufts. A common plant on acid moorland it makes a good spreader in a wildlife pool in boggy, shallow areas.
H 30–45cm (12–18in).
S indefinite. **PD** up to 5cm (2in).
Hardy. Full sun.

Glyceria maxima 'Variegata'
(Variegated water grass, sweet grass, manna grass)
Deciduous, spreading perennial grass with striking leaves which have stripes of cream-white and

green, often tinged with pink flushes at the base in spring and autumn. The flowers form greenish spikelets in summer. It spreads rapidly and must be kept in a container.
H 75cm (30in). **S** indefinite.
PD up to 15cm (6in).
Hardy. Full sun.

Houttuynia cordata
Deciduous perennial with clump-forming spreading roots and erect, leafy red stems bearing heart-shaped, pointed, highly aromatic, bluish green, leathery leaves. In spring spikes of insignificant flowers are produced surrounded by white bracts. Benefits from a leafy mulch in winter as the stems are borderline in hardiness. It is very invasive. The variety 'Chameleon' has leaves in a splash of bright hues: red and green splashed with yellow and cream.
H 15–60cm (6–24in). **S** indefinite.
PD no deeper than 2–5cm (1–2in).
Slightly tender. Semi-shade.

Iris laevigata (Water iris)
This deciduous perennial is one of the finest irises for shallow water. It

produces clumps of sword-shaped, soft green, smooth leaves without a midrib. The sparsely branched stem produces 2–4 broad petalled, beardless blue flowers. Can also be grown as a bog plant as long as it never dries out.
H 60–90cm (2–3ft). **S** indefinite.
PD up to 7–10cm (3–4in).
Hardy. Sun or semi-shade.

Iris pseudacorus (Flag iris)
A vigorous deciduous perennial with thick roots which will grow in shallow water or moist soil. The broad, sword-like, ridged leaves are grey-green with tall branched flower stems bearing as many as 10 beardless yellow flowers. The large, golden fall petals often have a darker patch in the centre. The variegated form is less vigorous and

produces bright cream-striped yellow leaves in spring.
H 1.5m (5ft). **S** indefinite.
PD 0–30cm (0–12in).
Hardy. Sun or shade.

Iris versicolor (Blue flag, wild iris)
Deciduous perennial which has clump-forming branched stems and sword-like narrow grey-green leaves. Each stems bears 3–5 violet-blue flowers with yellow patches at the petal bases and fall petals having a central white area and purple veins. It enjoys similar conditions to *I. laevigata* – permanent wet soil or a shallow covering of water.
H 60cm (2ft). **S** indefinite.
PD up to 5–7cm (2–3in).
Hardy. Semi-shade.

Lysichiton americanus
(Yellow skunk cabbage)
Vigorous deciduous aquatic which has bright yellow, arum-like, unpleasantly scented flowers in early spring before the impressive, heavily veined, architectural leaves, which can reach 1.2m (4ft). It needs a rich deep soil and should be protected

from cold winds and frost.
H 1.2m (4ft). **S** 75cm (30in).
PD 2–3cm (1in). Hardy. Full sun.

Lysichiton camtschatcensis
(Skunk cabbage)
Still vigorous but slightly more
compact than *L. americanus*, with
early spring flowers of pure white.
The paddle-like leaves are leathery,
oblong to oval, heavily veined and
bright green, produced in loose
rosettes. It is an excellent plant for
streamside planting in rich deep soil.
H 75cm (30in). **S** 60–90cm
(2–3ft). **PD** 2–3cm (1in).
Hardy. Full sun.

Menyanthes trifoliata
(Buckbean, bog bean, marsh trefoil)
Deciduous perennial with a thick
spongy creeping rootstock which
often floats on the water. The shiny,
clover-like olive green leaves are
made up of 3 leaflets with a long
leaf stalk which clasps the rhizome
with a broad sheath. Dainty, fringed
white to purplish flowers are
produced from pink buds on a
dense spike in spring.

H 22cm (9in). **S** indefinite.
PD 5cm (2in). Hardy. Full sun.

Myosotis scorpioides, syn. *M.
palustris* (Water forget-me-not)
Deciduous perennial which can be
found wild in Europe in shallow
mudbanks of still and slow-moving
water in marshy meadows, ditches
and ponds. The creeping rhizome
supports an angular stem which is
prostrate in the lower portions,
becoming erect at the tips. It forms
sprawling mounds of narrow mid-
green leaves 10cm (4in) long with
short rough hairs. It flowers in
loose racemes of small forget-me-
not, bright blue flowers which have
a central eye of pink, yellow or
white.
H 15–22cm (6–9in). **S** 30cm
(12in). **PD** up to 15cm (6in).
Hardy. Sun.

Peltandra virginica, syn.
P. undulata (Green arrow arum)
Deciduous perennial with narrowly
arrow-shaped, firm, bright green
leaves anywhere between 15 and
90cm (6–36in) long. The flowers

resemble small arum lilies, narrow
and strongly veined, 20cm (8in)
tall, which turn yellow or white
with waxy margins and are followed
by green berries in late summer.
H 1m (3ft). **S** 60cm (2ft).
PD 5–7cm (2–3in).
Hardy. Full sun.

Pontederia cordata (Pickerel weed)
A robust deciduous perennial, the
pickerel weed is one of the most
decorative blue-flowered aquatics.
The thick creeping root supports
leaves which are dark green, tidy
and erect with exquisite swirling. In
late summer dense spikes of soft
blue flowers are produced,
appearing from a leaf bract at the
top of the stem.
H 75cm (30in). **S** 45cm (18in).
PD 12cm (5in). Hardy. Full sun.

Sagittaria latifolia (American
arrowhead, duck potato, wapato)
Deciduous perennial with spreading
roots and soft green, arrow-shaped
leaves, sometimes reaching 80cm
(32in). The three-angled flower
stem carries the white flowers in

summer. Produces overwintering walnut-sized tubers at the ends of the roots which become detached in the autumn. An excellent plant for the wildlife pool.
H 1.5m (5ft). **S** 60cm (2ft). **PD** 15cm (6in).
Hardy. Full sun.

Sagittaria sagittifolia
(Common arrowhead)
Deciduous perennial with a short branching root and acutely arrow-shaped leaves. In summer three-petalled white flowers appear in spikes on triangular flower stems with the upper male flowers on the spike having a violet centre. It prefers shallow water, flowering will be restricted in water deeper than 15cm (6in).
H 45cm (18in).
S 30cm (12in).
Hardy. Full sun.

Saururus cernuus (Lizard's tail, swamp lily, water dragon)
Deciduous perennial with clump forming erect stems bearing heart-shaped, bright green leaves.

The flowers are nodding spikes of waxy, fragrant creamy flowers in summer. It makes a distinctive specimen when planted slightly away from the margins to allow the leaves and flowers to be surrounded by water.
H 22cm (9in). **S** 30cm (12in).
PD 10–15cm (4–6in).
Hardy. Full sun.

Schoenoplectus lacustris subsp. *tabernaemontani* 'Zebrinus'
(Club rush, zebra rush)
Despite its cumbersome name, this is a splendid plant, often still labelled *Scirpus*. A spreading perennial sedge with a strong root that creeps along the soil surface, it has erect, leafless stems in a dark green with cream horizontal banding like porcupine quills. The flowers are white and brown terminal spikelets in summer. A dramatic plant which needs a dark background to show off the unusual leaf banding.
H 1.5m (5ft). **S** indefinite.
PD 7–15cm (3–6in).
Hardy. Full sun.

Scrophularia auriculata 'Variegata' (Water figwort)
Evergreen, clump-forming perennial, with stiff square stems carrying nettle-like leaves with creamy margins and a light green centre. The smaller leaves are almost entirely cream. Spikes of insignificant greenish-purple flowers are held above the foliage and much appreciated by bees.
H 1m (3ft). **S** 60cm (2ft).
PD 7cm (3in). Hardy. Full sun.

Typha minima (Dwarf reedmace)
The common reedmace (almost always, but wrongly, called a bullrush), is a thug of a plant, but this miniature version is perfect for a very small pool. In late summer and through the autumn its distinctive chocolate brown seedheads appear among the thin grassy foliage.
H 45–60cm (18–24in).
S 30cm (12in). Hardy. Full sun.

Veronica beccabunga (Brooklime)
Semi-evergreen, perennial scrambler with rather succulent, hollow

creeping stems which root as they scramble over the wet soil. The short-stalked, fleshy leaves have blue flowers with white centres borne in their axils. An excellent scrambler for the edge and a mud bottom, but inclined to become straggly.

H 10cm (4in). **S** indefinite. **PD** 7cm (3in). Hardy. Full sun.

Zantedeschia aethiopica
'Crowborough'
(Arum lily, calla lily)
A robust marginal which in summer produces a succession of familiar fragrant arum-like flowers 8–25cm (3–10in) long with a central yellow poker. The white flowers are set off by shiny, arrow-shaped leaves of deep green. This cultivar is hardier than the species and will survive outdoors in a temperate winter provided it is covered with 30cm (12in) of water. The spathes of *Z. aethiopica* 'Green Goddess' are green with a large central green-splashed white area. Both vareieties are excellent in a formal setting.

H 45–90cm (1½–3ft). **S** 35–45cm (14–18in). **PD** 30cm (12in). Min. temp 10°C (50°F) when not covered with water, otherwise hardy. Full sun.

MOISTURE-LOVING PLANTS

Moisture-loving, or bog, plants grow in the damp soil just above the water line around the pool. These plants require a permanently moist soil, but with free drainage – they will not tolerate waterlogging for any period. Around an informal pool this condition can achieved by providing an area of soil around the margins which is kept moist by the wet soil underneath, allowing the plants to dip into this reserve for their summer requirements. Alternatively, you can create a bog garden (see pages 28–9).

The range of plants suited to these conditions plays a very important part in the natural transition from the normal soil to the aquatic conditions of the pool. Many herbaceous plants,

traditionally grown in the herbaceous border, will excel in this 'fringe' environment, producing a vigour and lushness which is seldom exhibited in normal soil in high summer.

Ajuga reptans 'Multicolor'
(Carpet bugle)
A hardy evergreen perennial which spreads freely by runners forming a colourful creeper. This variety has short spikes of blue flowers and purple bracts carried just above the variegated leaves which are in shades of bronze pink with gold splashes.

H 10–12cm (4–5in). **S** 45cm (18in). Hardy. Sun or shade.

Astilbe x 'Arendsii'
Summer-flowering, herbaceous perennial with plumes of flowers in a wide variety of pinks, reds and white. The dark green foliage, divided into ferny leaflets, has coppery tints when young. New introductions continue to extend the range available.

H 45–60cm (18–24in). S 1m (3ft). Hardy. Partial shade.

Caltha palustris
(Marsh marigold)
An appealing perennial happy in boggy ground or shallow water. It has rich green, rounded leaves on branching stems. The spring flowers are like large, shiny buttercups (it is sometimes called the kingcup). 'Flore Pleno' is a very showy double variety.
H 30–40cm (12–16in). S 22–30cm (9–12in). Hardy. Sun.

Cardamine pratensis
(Cuckoo flower)
Perennial forming tufts of cress-like foliage and rosy-lilac flowers that look well near wildlife pools. The form 'Flore Pleno' has double flowers.
H 30–45cm (12–18in). S 30cm (12in). Hardy. Full sun.

Carex elata 'Aurea', syn. *C. stricta* 'Aurea' (Bowles' golden sedge)
Dense tuft-forming perennial sedge which makes colourful foliage in the wet soil at the water's edge and at the same time provides a textural contrast to wider leaved plants. The solid triangular stems bear blackish-brown spikelets which are rather inconspicuous in the grassy golden yellow leaves in summer. Although happy in shallow water, it succeeds best in moist soil that is never allowed to dry out.
H 40–90cm (16–36in). S 1m (3ft). Hardy. Full sun.

Carex pendula (Pendulous sedge)
An evergreen perennial with tufts of narrow, grass like green leaves. Triangular stalks 1m (3ft) long support pendulous spikes of brown flowers which are extremely effective when reflected in the water surface. This species will also succeed in very shallow water.
H 60–90cm (2–3ft). S 1.5m (5ft). Hardy. Sun or shade.

Crocosmia 'Lucifer'
Clump-forming perennial growing from corms with slender swords of bright green leaves. The flame-red, trumpet-shaped flowers are eye-

catching in late summer, supported on dense, branching spikes.
H 1.2m (4ft). S 25–30cm (10–12in). Hardy. Full sun.

Darmera peltata (Umbrella plant)
Distinctive perennial producing round, umbrella-like leaves 30–45cm (12–18in) across on single stems. The pinky white flowers appear before the leaves on single stems 60cm (24in) high in spring. The thick surface roots help prevent erosion at the poolside.
H 1m (3ft). S 60cm (2ft). Hardy. Full sun.

Hemerocallis (Day lily)

The reliable display of trumpet-shaped flowers make the day lilies very popular. Dwarf forms, such as the bright yellow-flowered 'Stella d'Oro', grow no higher than 40cm (16in), while 'Golden Chimes', with deep yellow flowers, grows over twice as tall. Colours range from a creamy white through every shade of yellow, gold and orange to a rich tawny and deep claret; there are also a few peaches and pinks. **H** 60–90cm (2–3ft). **S** 60–90cm (2–3ft). Hardy. Full sun.

Hosta (Plantain lily)

The numerous species and varieties of this genus offer a wide variety of colour, texture and variegation in their broad, handsome leaves, making a lush display at any poolside. They vary in size from the aptly named *H.* 'Tiny Tears', to imposing stands of *H. sieboldiana*. **H** 22–60cm (9–24in). **S** 30–90cm (1–3ft). Hardy. Partial shade.

Iris

Several species enjoy the moist soil, particularly the exotic *I. ensata* (formerly *I. kaempferi*), with its large, boldly marked, clematis-like flowers in several shades, and its broad, sword-like leaves with a distinct midrib. **H** 75cm (2½ft). **S** 30cm (12in). Hardy. Sun.

I. sibirica

Another good species for moist soil with much more slender, grass-like leaves than most other irises and branching flower heads of various shades, often with blue or purple veining in the petals. **H** 60–120cm (2–4ft). **S** 1m (3ft). Hardy. Sun or partial shade.

Ligularia przewalskii 'The Rocket'

An attractive member of a varied genus of large-leaved, clump-forming herbaceous perennials. It is distinguished by its jagged-edged, round, dark green leaves on very dark stems. In late summer it produces narrow spikes of small, lemon yellow daisy-like flowers. They benefit from a mulch over deep fertile soils to prevent them from wilting on bright windy days. They are most effective planted in large groups. **H** 1.2–1.8m (4–6ft). **S** 1m (3ft). Hardy. Full sun.

Lobelia cardinalis (Cardinal flower)

Clump-forming perennial with rosettes of oval leaves which vary from fresh green to reddish bronze. The striking flower spikes appear in late summer ranging in various shades of bright red and deep scarlet. It should have a protective mulch to overwinter the plant if kept *in situ*, or it can be lifted and then overwintered in cold frames. **H** 1m (3ft). **S** 30cm (12in). Slightly tender. Full sun.

Osmunda regalis (Regal fern)
An elegant deciduous fern with bright green, leathery, divided fronds which turn to a rusty red in the autumn. Brown fertile flower spikes appear at the tips of taller fronds when the plant is mature.
H 1.5–1.8m (5–6ft). **S** 1m (3ft). Hardy. Partial shade.

Primula beesiana

A candelabra type primula with rough-textured leaves and rich purple flowers with yellow eyes. The flowers can vary from rich mauve to deep carmine.
H 60cm (2ft). **S** 30cm (12in). Hardy. Sun or partial shade.

P. bulleyana
A candelabra primula with dark green, thin, toothed leaves and orange-yellow flowers growing on strong stalks.

H 60–90cm (2–3ft). **S** 45cm (18in). Hardy. Sun or partial shade.

P. denticulata
A drumstick primula and one of the earliest to flower, it has round flower heads of lilac to rich carmine-red on stout stems. The toothed leaves are broadly lance-shaped.
H 22–30cm (9–12in). **S** 30cm (12in). Hardy. Sun.

P. florindae
One of the most vigorous of the waterside primulas, producing several heads of large drooping, sulphur yellow, bell-like flowers covered with a white mealy powder. The large heart-shaped leaves can reach up to 20cm (8in) long.
H 75cm (2½ft). **S** 60cm (2ft). Hardy. Sun or partial shade.

P. japonica
A showy candelabra type, ideal for group planting. The stout flower stems bear dense tiers of white, red, pink or crimson flower, above pale green, lance-shaped leaves with a bluish tint. 'Millers Crimson' is a

good dark red and 'Postford White' an excellent white variety.
H 30–60cm (2–3ft). **S** 30cm (12in). Hardy. Sun or partial shade.

P. prolifera
A bold, yellow-flowered candelabra type which is similar to *P. florindae* but lacks the mealy powder on the flower spikes. The long, pale green leaves have toothed edges.
H 1m (3ft). **S** 45cm (18in). Hardy. Sun or partial shade.

P. pulverulenta
An elegant candelabra type with bold tiers of rich crimson, purple-eyed flowers on a spike covered in mealy powder. The wrinkled leaves are lance-shaped with toothed edges.
H 60cm (2ft). **S** 30cm (12in). Hardy. Sun or partial shade.

P. rosea
An early-flowering polyanthus-like flower head of rose pink supported on short stalks above oval to lance-shaped leaves.
H 10–15cm (4–6in). **S** 15cm (6in). Hardy. Full sun.

Rheum palmatum
(Ornamental rhubarb)
Stout, clump-forming perennial with a tough woody rhizome, the rheum is grown for its foliage and architectural merit. The large leaves are rounded, five-lobed and deeply cut. In early summer, impressive spikes of small flowers appear, in shades of cream, pink or red according to variety, with the seedheads adding a later attraction. The various forms hybridize readily, but a particularly striking form is *R. palmatum* 'Atrosanguineum', with new stems and leaves a rich red-purple. The colour remains on the undersides of the leaves as they mature and the flowers are a vivid crimson.
H 2m (6ft). **S** 2m (6ft).
Hardy. Sun or semi-shade.

Rodgersia podophylla
Clump-forming, rhizomatous perennial grown for its attractive large leaves with jagged lobes. These have bronzy veining when young, later become green and then take on copper tints. The densely clustered panicles of tiny flowers which appear in late summer are creamy white, occasionally pink. It must have shelter from wind and makes a good substitute for the giant gunnera in a smaller garden.
H 1.2m (4ft). **S** 1m (3ft).
Hardy. Sun or semi-shade.

Senecio smithii
Bushy herbaceous perennial with thick woolly stems clothed with spear-shaped, shiny dark green leaves about 45cm (18in) long. Held above the leaves are plumes of white daisy-like flowers about 2–3cm (1in) in diameter. These appear in early summer and are followed by clusters of fluffy white seedheads.
H 1–1.2m (3–4ft).
S 75–90cm (2½–3ft).
Hardy. Sun or semi-shade.

Trollius europaeus (Globe flower)
A compact perennial which resembles a large double buttercup with lemon yellow flowers with incurved petals growing above heavily dissected, buttercup-like leaves.
H 60cm (2ft). **S** 60cm (2ft).
Hardy. Sun or partial shade.

INDEX

Page numbers in *italic* refer to
the illustrations

Photograph Acknowledgements

John Glover 6 (Horticultural Therapy), 10, 14(l) (Hampstead Horticultural Society), 16 (Dale Stone Co.), 37 (Mark Walker), 60, 63, 64, 71 (Home Farm Trust), 72, 80. **Jerry Harpur** 2 (Design: Raymond Hudson, Johannesburg), 5 (Design: Denis Lochen, Spain), 17 (Design: Sonny Garcia, San Francisco), 52 (Design: Mark Peter Keane, Kyoto), 55 (Design: Leslie Smith, Johannesburg), 56 (Design: Robert Watson, New Zealand), 74 (Design: Raymond Hudson, Johannesburg), 86 (Design: Denis Lochen, Spain), 88 (Japanese Stroll Garden, New York), 92 (Design: Mark Rumary, Suffolk), 104 (Design: Jim Matsuo, Los Angeles), 105 (Design: Robin Williams, Berks). **Sunniva Harte/Garden Picture Library** 91, 103,/ **Pots and Pithoi** 100. Andrew Lawson 1 (Chelsea Flower Show '95. Design: Rupert Golby), 7, 13, 58, (Whichford Pottery, Warks). **Marianne Majerus** 14(r), 15, 69, 76, 82, 97. **S & O Mathews** 3, 114

and 125 (Merrie Cottage, Hants); 30 and 109 (RHS Garden, Wisley); 61 and 119 (Cobblers, Sussex); 90 (Shepherds, Kent), 102, 123, 124. **Clive Nichols** 10 (Design: Julian Dowle), 36 (Design: C & J Nichols), 85 (Design: Julian Dowle & K Ninomiya), 98. **Harry Smith Collection** 9, 78. **Derek St Romaine** 8 (RHS Chelsea Show '96 'A Garden of Reflection'. Design: Hiroshi Nanamori & Andrew Butcher), 11 (Cleve West's garden. Design: Cleve West & Johnny Woodford), 12, 20 (Mark Rumary's garden. Design: Mark Rumary), 28 and 40 (Maureen Thompson), 45, 68 (RHS Chelsea Show '95 'Evening Standard Eros garden'. Design: Julie Toll), 77 (RHS Hampton Court Show '95 'Scenic Design Landscaping'. Design: Christopher Costin), 83 (Maureen Thompson), 94 (Design: Richard Sales), 96 and 107 (RHS Chelsea Show '96 'Living Rooms'. Design: Roger Platts).